The Art of Saying No

While Staying in the Will of God

The Art of Saying No

While Staying in the Will of God

Zaneta Adams

Grace Under Fire Publishing

Published by Grace Under Fire Publishing Muskegon, Michigan

Scripture quotations are taken from the Holy Bible, New International Version®, NIV®. Copyright @ 1973, 1978, 1984, 2011 by Biblica, Inc.™ Used by permission of Zondervan. All rights reserved worldwide.

Some names and identifying details have been changed to protect the privacy of individuals.

Copy edited by Geoffrey Stone

ISBN: 979-8-9956951-0-3

Library of Congress Control Number: 2026912790

First Edition

Printed in the United States of America

To my husband, Joseph — my rock. I love you.

This book exists because you held everything up while I figured out how to put some things down. Your support, your patience, and your steadfast presence made publication possible. I could not have done this without you.

To my mother and my grandmother —

You were the first women who showed me what strength looked like, and the first to love me before I knew what I was becoming. Everything I know about endurance, I learned watching you.

To the man who chose to be my dad —

You didn't have to say yes. But you said yes to my mother, and in doing so, you said yes to all of us. In a book about the weight of a yes, I could not leave that one unacknowledged. Thank you for choosing us.

To my daughters —

You put up with me while I figured it all out. You watched me navigate life in real time — the missteps, the overcommitments, the slow and sometimes messy work of becoming. You never stopped believing in me, even when I hadn't yet become the mother I was working toward being for you. I hope this book shows you that the work was always, in part, for you.

To my mother-in-law, my sisters, my brother, my aunts, and my closest friends —

You encouraged me when I needed it, supported me when I doubted, and — when I said yes one too many times and buried myself under the weight of it — you told me the truth. Not because it was easy, but because you loved me enough not to stay quiet. That honesty, offered with courage, held up a mirror I didn't know I needed. It helped me see the busyness I had mistaken for godliness — and in seeing it clearly, find the words for this book.

To my sons —

You are the reason saying no has always mattered. Every boundary I learned to hold was, in part, me learning how to show up more fully for you. I pray this book leaves you something worth carrying.

And to every woman who was told her no didn't matter — it does.

Foreword

by Tonya L. Moore

I have known Zaneta Adams since 2014. And I want to be very clear about what that means.

I met her the same month she founded WINC: For All Women Veterans—before the organization had a stage, before it had a scholarship, before it had a name that people recognized. I was still at BET Networks at the time and had just released my own book. Two women, both stepping into something new, both figuring out what it meant to say yes to the thing God had placed in front of them. I didn't know then how long we would walk together. I just knew she was serious about what she was building.

I knew her before the appointments and the accolades. Before the cabinet position, before the stages, before the national headlines. And when she told me she was writing this book, I wasn't surprised. I had watched her live it.

I remember the first call.

She had been offered a position in Washington, DC. It was the kind of opportunity that most people would have said yes to before the conversation was over. I was living in Baltimore at the time, and I told her without hesitation—if you take it, I've got you. My home was open. Whatever she needed to make the transition work, we would figure it out together.

Then came the second call. She didn't lead with an explanation. She didn't have to. I heard it before she said a word—something in her voice that had nothing to do with logistics. She wasn't calling to think it through. She was calling to say she wouldn't need the room.

She said no to DC.

What I know is this: that was not an easy call to make. And the woman on the other end of that phone had made it anyway.

But here is what I want you to understand about Zaneta Adams. That decision was not an isolated moment. It was a pattern. A discipline. A woman actively learning, in real time, how to align her decisions with God's voice instead of the world's applause.

I watched her build WINC from the ground up. I had the honor of serving as Master of Ceremonies for the HERR2 Awards—her signature recognition event celebrating women veterans—and I watched that room fill with women whose lives had been touched by what she was building. WINC gave me something I did not expect: it gave me a scholarship. I was the organization's first and only scholarship recipient. So when I say I have watched this woman give, I am not speaking from the outside. I am one of the women she poured into.

And last October, I got on a plane and flew to Michigan to watch her receive the Hall of Honor award for her work in the veterans space. I sat in that room and I thought about the woman I met in 2014—the one who said yes to everything, who ran herself ragged out of love and obligation and a deep need to be needed—and I watched her be honored for the very work she had protected by finally learning to say no. The no she said to DC. The no she said to the opportunities that would have taken her away from her assignment. The no that made room for everything in that room.

I was proud. I will not pretend otherwise.

I founded Bravery Park to serve homeless women veterans—women who have given everything and found themselves with nowhere to land. Zaneta is part of that work because I believe in her, and because she has earned it. And that mission is only possible because she protected her assignment long enough to see it become something that can now protect someone else. That is the through line of this book. And it is the through line of her life.

What Zaneta has done in these pages is rare. She does not preach from a distance. She pulls from her own story—from the trauma, the overcommitment, the seasons when yes was a hiding place and no felt impossible—and she turns all of it into wisdom you can actually use. She is honest about what it cost her to learn this. And she is generous enough to put it in your hands so it does not have to cost you the same.

As a veteran, I know what it means to operate in environments where every instinct tells you to keep moving. As a survivor, I know what it means when your own voice has been silenced—and how long the road back to trusting it can be. And as a woman of faith who has done her own work of becoming, I know that the hardest nos are not the ones we say to other people. They are the ones we say to the version of ourselves that was built to survive rather than to live.

This book will ask you to say that no. And it will hold your hand while you do.

I have watched Zaneta Adams say yes when she should have, and no when it mattered most. I have watched her remain the same woman at the root of every title, every stage, every honor. I have watched her build, serve, sacrifice, and still—somehow—stay grounded in who God called her to be.

That woman wrote this book. And I am honored to call her my friend, my sister, my fellow veteran, and one of the clearest examples I know of a life lived in the will of God.

Read every word. Do every reflection. Pray every prayer.

And then—finally—say no to what was never yours to carry.

Tonya L. Moore

Author, I'm All F*d Up: The Story of My Life

U.S. Air National Guard Veteran | Founder & CEO, Bravery Park

Former Corporate Relations Manager, BET Networks

Contents

Choosing to Decide

From our earliest days, we learn that the word no is often associated with discipline, denial, and sometimes rejection. It is a word that stops us, corrects us, and occasionally wounds us. For many of us, it carries emotional weight far beyond its two small letters.

For many women—and particularly for women who have lived limitations—no has not always been protective. It has been used to deny opportunity, silence voices, restrict movement, and enforce roles without consent. As recently as the 1970s, many women could not access credit without a male cosigner, and that legacy of rejection still lingers across generations.

So when we are told no—especially from authority, from systems, or even from God—it can feel not just disappointing, but personal. It can feel disrespectful, unsafe, and even stir fear that obedience will lead to loss rather than freedom.

However, Scripture tells a different story.

Now anyone who knows me is probably reading the title of this book and thinking, Has she mastered the art of saying no? Nah, she's the queen of yes. And honestly, they wouldn't be wrong. At least until now.

For a long time, I lived at a pace that rewarded availability and productivity. Saying yes felt responsible. It felt faithful. And the world applauded it. What the applause never acknowledged was the quiet cost: the erosion of peace, the fraying of relationships, and the spiritual exhaustion that comes from constantly responding instead of being discerning.

I didn't feel rebellious. I felt busy. I didn't feel disobedient. I felt needed. And being needed felt righteous. But I didn't realize how far I had drifted from stillness until stopping felt uncomfortable.

Jesus often used parables to reveal deeper spiritual truths, and one of the most profound lessons on discernment comes from the parable of the ten virgins:

The foolish ones said to the wise, 'Give us some of your oil; our lamps are going out.' 'No,' they replied, 'there may not be enough for both us and you. Instead, go to those who sell oil and buy some for yourselves.' (Matthew 25:8–9)

At first blush, their refusal probably seemed harsh. In a moment of urgency, their no felt abrupt. But here is the thing we fail to grasp: their no was not rooted in selfishness—it was rooted in wisdom.

Have you ever had a group project in school or at work? There is almost always a weak link. There's that one person who doesn't show up to the planning meetings, doesn't complete their portion, or waits until the last minute and hopes someone else will cover for them. And almost without fail, there is also that other person—the gap-filler, the rescuer, the one who steps in so the group doesn't fail.

But here's the uncomfortable question: How does anyone gain wisdom if the consequences are always absorbed by someone else? What if instead of filling the gap we simply completed our portion and let the instructor see the truth? The person who failed to prepare would be dealt with accordingly. And you would have fulfilled your responsibility without carrying what was never yours to hold.

That is exactly what the wise virgins did. They prepared. They understood their assignment. And they knew their responsibility was not to rescue others from a lack of preparation but to remain faithful to what they had been given.

This parable reminds us of a truth we often resist: Saying no is sometimes necessary to protect what God has entrusted to us. Stewardship requires discernment. Faithfulness sometimes looks like restraint.

Hear me when I say this: The ability to say no is not weakness. It is wisdom in action. It is the willingness to protect the purpose God placed in you rather than appease the pressure people place on you.

There is a Scripture I have carried with me for years—one I return to whenever I need to remember not just what I am doing but why:

The Spirit of the Lord is on me, because he has anointed me to proclaim good news to the poor. He has sent me to proclaim freedom for the prisoners and recovery of sight for the blind, to set the oppressed free. (Luke 4:18)

I believe this book is part of that commission for me. Not because I have arrived. But because I have watched too many women—women of faith, women of strength, women who love God deeply—live bruised and bound because they were never taught to use a two-letter word with confidence.

So when I say this book is an invitation, I mean that with everything in me. An invitation to healing, to truth, to the kind of freedom that does not require you to explain yourself or apologize for becoming who God made you to be.

A Note on How to Use This Book

At the end of every chapter you will find reflection questions and a prayer. The questions are designed to help you examine honestly, strengthen your resolve, and move toward what God is asking of you. Grab a journal—some of what surfaces during these pages deserves more than a moment's thought. The prayers are written for the moments when your own words feel too heavy to carry.

Practical Exercise

As you begin this journey, consider this: Where in your life have you learned to say yes automatically, without discernment? What might change if obedience—not pressure—became the measure of your faithfulness?

Take a few quiet moments and journal about a time when saying yes left you feeling overwhelmed, depleted, or misaligned.

What did that yes cost you? What might a well-placed no have protected?

PRAYER

Lord, open my heart to what I have been avoiding about the word no. I come to You not from a place of mastery, but from a place of hunger—hungry for the kind of wisdom that does not chase urgency, does not perform availability, and does not measure faithfulness by how exhausted I become.

Teach me to see my worth clearly. Not through how much I produce, how quickly I respond, or how often I am needed—but through the truth that I am already held, already loved, and already called. Show me where I have confused my pace with my purpose and where what I have thought was obligation was really just fear.

As I begin this journey, I am asking You to do the deep work first. Bring to the surface what I have buried. Reveal what I have avoided. And speak into the silence that I have been too busy to sit in. Grant me the wisdom to discern when to say no, the courage to obey You even when it is uncomfortable, and the faith to trust that Your boundaries are not limitations—but are the shape of love itself.

In Jesus' mighty name, amen.

My Reflections

Personal notes from the Introduction

CHAPTER ONE

Where No Begins

Do you remember the first time you heard the word no?

Maybe it was your mother's voice—firm, immediate, and non-negotiable. "No. Don't touch that."

Maybe it was a teacher delivering your first reprimand in front of the class, the kind that stung more than it should have. "No, that's not how we do it."

Or maybe it was the first time someone told you no, and it didn't just stop you, it hurt.

I can't honestly say I remember the very first time I heard the word "no." But I'm fairly confident it happened long before I could walk. In our house, "no" was not a suggestion. It was a full sentence. There was no bargaining, no softening, and absolutely no pretending it hadn't been said.

Like most of us, I learned no early—long before I understood its purpose, long before I could appreciate its protection, and long before I could tell the difference between being rejected and being restrained.

Most people don't like hearing no. We want to do things when we want to do them and how we want to do them. And when no stands in the way, it often feels like denial instead of direction.

What we rarely recognize in the moment is that no is often used to protect us—from something or someone we cannot see clearly.

The problem is that protection doesn't always feel good. Take teenagers, for example.

I can still picture the looks on my children's faces when they heard the word no, the look they gave me when they wanted to stay up just a little longer, play one more video game, or go to that party I already knew I was going to say no to before they finished the sentence. To them, no felt unfair. It felt restrictive. It felt like I was standing in the way of their independence, and to hear them tell it, possibly their entire future.

Most of the time, I said no because something didn't sit right with me. Sometimes I said no because homework wasn't done or chores weren't completed. And if I'm being honest, sometimes I couldn't fully explain it. I just knew yes wasn't the right answer.

What they experienced as control, I understood as care, and what they felt as restriction and unfairness, I recognized as protection.

Still, I get why no stings—because I've been on the receiving end of it too.

Love without boundaries is not love. It's avoidance wearing a kinder name.

Somewhere early in life, "no" becomes embedded in us as something negative, almost like a bad word. It interrupts pleasure. It challenges autonomy. It makes us feel small, powerless, or unseen. Over time, we start associating "no" with loss instead of love.

That conditioning follows us into adulthood. So to combat how we feel, we soften no. We apologize for it. We overexplain it, and sometimes we refuse to say it at all.

You see this clearly in parenting. The parents who avoid saying no don't usually do so out of wisdom. They do it out of discomfort. They don't want to be the "bad guy." They worry that boundaries might stifle creativity or independence. But more often than not, the parent not wanting to say no has less to do with the child and more to do with the parent's need to be liked.

Saying no is hard when you want approval. It's hard when you want to avoid conflict, and it's hard when love gets confused with acceptance. Having raised six children, I said no much more with my older kids than with my younger ones. Why? Because I don't have as much energy or patience to deal with the drama no causes as I did then.

But Scripture is blunt about this tension:

Whoever spares the rod hates their children, but the one who loves their children is careful to discipline them. (Proverbs 13:24)

Love without boundaries is not love. It's avoidance wearing a kinder name.

No as Protection

The word "no" didn't originate with parents, teachers, or authority figures. It has existed as long as humanity itself. Linguists trace it back to ancient roots—simple sounds meaning "not," "never," or "refusal." Variations of "no" appear across nearly every language and culture.

Long before laws or contracts were written, the word "no" existed. And long before institutions or theology, humans needed a way to stop, to resist, to refuse, and to protect. Hence the full sentence No. No is a boundary word and statement, and boundaries are not modern inventions. They are ancient necessities.

One of the earliest—and most revealing—examples of the power of no appears in the garden of Eden.

God's instruction to Adam and Eve was clear: Do not eat from the tree of the knowledge of good and evil (Genesis 2:17). This was not a suggestion. It was a boundary designed to protect humanity from something they were not equipped to handle.

The tragedy wasn't that Eve heard "no"; it was that she stopped believing it was good.

When the serpent introduced doubt—Did God really say?—belief fractured. Once belief fractured, obedience collapsed. The sin in Eden was not merely disobedience; it was disbelief. Eve did not trust that God's boundary was for her benefit, and Adam did not believe God's word strongly enough to intervene.

God's first no was not cruel nor was it controlling. It was protective.

Humanity's first mistake was not hearing "no"; it was believing the lie that no was withholding something good.

The Bible does not shy away from "no." In fact, depending on the translation, the word "no"—and its derivatives "not," "do not," "shall not"—appears hundreds of times explicitly and thousands of times by implication.

From "You shall have no other gods before Me" to "You shall not steal," Scripture consistently uses "no" to establish moral clarity, covenant level faithfulness, and relational stability.

Jesus Himself reinforced this principle when He said, "All you need to say is simply 'Yes' or 'No'; anything beyond this comes from the evil one" (Matthew 5:37).

Clarity is not cruelty, boundaries are not betrayal, and "no" is not the enemy of faith; it is often its guardian.

No as Redirection

Let's face it. There's no denying that "no" has caused pain.

We've heard "no" when we wanted approval, "no" when we wanted opportunity, "no" when we wanted love, and "no" when we were convinced we were ready—even though we weren't. Some of those moments still hurt.

But if we're brave enough to look back, many of the "nos" that once devastated us also redirected us. They spared us relationships that would have broken us. They closed doors we weren't meant to walk through. They delayed plans that would have collapsed under their own weight.

In their hearts humans plan their course, but the Lord establishes their steps. —Proverbs 16:9

Sometimes what feels like rejection is actually mercy doing its quiet work. And sometimes the problem isn't that we heard too many "nos." It's that we ignored them.

When No Becomes Your Own to Give

For years, I struggled with saying "no." I said yes despite exhaustion, despite lack of desire, and despite running on fumes. I told myself I was helping people. I told myself I was serving others. I told myself it was the right thing to do.

All that sounds noble—until you add context.

I was raising multiple sets of twins and two singletons. I had a husband. I had a career. I had responsibilities stacked so high I'm honestly surprised I was able to still see daylight. If you're wondering how that math works, trust me—it doesn't. I was never home.

What I didn't realize then was that my inability to say "no" wasn't out of the desire to be holy. It was out of habit. And that habit was costing me the very things I was trying to protect.

Many of the joys we carry today exist because something else was denied. Either a relationship that didn't last, a door that never opened, or a plan that fell apart.

But—here we are. Still standing, still growing and still becoming.

The first job I applied for after passing the bar exam was for a firm where I had interned. I loved the work, and I believed I had been an effective intern. In my mind, this was the natural next step. So when they told me "no," I was devastated. I remember thinking, Surely, they need to rethink this decision. Surely this is a mistake.

But the no stood.

What I didn't know at the time was that God was already opening a different door—one I never would have pursued if that first yes had come through.

With unexpected time on my hands, I decided to coach my daughter's high school mock trial team. A friend graciously allowed me to use a conference room at her law firm for practices. While I was there, I met the firm's senior partner.

After a few conversations, he hired me.

That role ended up stretching across multiple areas of law, which turned out to be exactly what I, as someone with a bit of a squirrel mentality, needed. More importantly, my nonprofit work wasn't just tolerated at that firm, it was supported and encouraged. I was given the freedom to serve in other spaces while still growing professionally.

That job gave me exposure, flexibility, and credibility I would not have had otherwise. It became a launching point for opportunities and leadership roles I couldn't see at the time—roles we'll talk about later in this book.

While the door that closed felt like rejection, it was actually redirection.

God wasn't withholding something good—He was making room for something better suited to who I was becoming.

And just like God had plans for me that I couldn't see then, He has plans for you too—even in the "no" that still stings. He said it best in Jeremiah 29:11: "For I know the plans I have for you, declares the Lord, plans to prosper you and not to harm you, plans to give you hope and a future."

Just like with my story, sometimes "no" isn't the end of the story. It's the full sentence that leads to the next chapter.

Take a moment to sit with the very first memory you have of hearing the word no. As a child you couldn't rationalize it; you simply felt it. Were you hurt, confused, relieved, or afraid? What did that moment quietly teach you about authority, about your worth, about whether your desires mattered to anyone other than you? We often carry our earliest experiences of no into every relationship and decision we make as adults without ever recognizing where the pattern began. Can you trace it? Can you name the first time you learned that your no might not be safe?

Think about a more recent no—a door that closed, an opportunity that didn't come, a relationship that ended before you were ready. What story did you tell yourself in the aftermath? Did you hear rejection, or were you able, even partially, to trust that God was redirecting something? If there is a no in your past that you have never fully brought to God, this is the invitation to do that now—not to demand an explanation but to lay it down.

Finally, consider this: How has your relationship with receiving no shaped the way you give it? Do you apologize for it, soften it, over-explain it, or avoid saying it entirely to keep the peace? Is there a specific relationship—name it, don't let it stay vague—where your no has never fully landed with authority? Where you are still waiting for someone else's permission before your own decision feels final? What would it look like to practice saying no once this week without going back on it?

Lord, teach me to trust "no" as protection, not as rejection. Where I have received a no that still hurts, I bring it to You now. Not for explanation but for peace. Not for reversal but for the kind of understanding that only comes through surrender.

Help me release the nos that still feel personal. The closed doors, the unanswered prayers, the seasons that did not go the way I believed they would. I confess that I have sometimes read Your silence as absence, and Your redirection as rejection. Heal what those misreadings have quietly built in me.

And as I learn to carry this truth, teach me to use "no" with the same wisdom and love You have used with me. Let my refusals not wound the people I love but protect what You have entrusted to both of us. Let "no" in my mouth become an act of faith, not an act of fear.

In Jesus' mighty name, amen.

My Reflections

Personal notes from Chapter One

When God Says No—and Our Faith Wavers

Trigger Warning
This chapter includes a personal reflection involving sexual assault and its emotional and spiritual aftermath. These experiences are shared with care—not to retraumatize, but to tell the truth about how God restores belief after pain. Please engage at your own pace and seek support if needed.

Faith is not simply believing that God exists. Faith is believing what God says.

That difference matters more than we may realize.

Most of us don't struggle because we haven't heard God. We struggle because at some point we stopped trusting what He said—especially when it became uncomfortable, confusing, or painful.

As discussed earlier, from the very beginning, humanity's struggle has never been about clarity. God has always been clear. In the garden of Eden, He did not speak vaguely or leave room for confusion. He gave a direct instruction: Do not eat from the tree of the knowledge of good and evil. He even explained why. The boundary was obvious. The consequence was stated plainly.

What failed was not understanding. What failed was belief.

When Belief and Trust Come Apart

Here's where many of us get tangled. Belief is accepting that God's word is true. Trust is believing it is good for you. Obedience is operating as if both are true.

You can believe Scripture and still struggle to trust it. But when trust breaks, obedience becomes incredibly hard.

That's why people can quote Bible verses and still ignore what God is telling them to do. It's not because they don't know better. It's because something inside them doesn't feel safe enough to follow through.

When we stop believing that God's "no" is protective, we begin treating it as restrictive. And once that happens, "no" starts to feel cruel instead of caring.

Throughout Scripture, God also uses "no" to protect relationship, not control it. The commandments are not cages—they are guardrails. They were meant to keep people from falling off cliffs they couldn't yet see.

Jesus modeled this perfectly. When tempted in the wilderness, He didn't negotiate. He didn't explain Himself. He didn't test how close He could get without crossing the line. He said "no" and stood on truth.

In the garden before the cross, He prayed, "Not my will, but Yours be done." That was not weakness. That was trust.

When belief erodes, we start reasoning our way around conviction. We explain. We justify. We delay. And we convince ourselves that God will understand, all while quietly stepping outside the boundary He already set.

And usually the cost shows up later.

The Cost of Disbelief

Samson knew his calling. He wasn't confused. His life was marked from birth. The boundaries were clear, and God didn't hide them.

But Samson had a problem that didn't look like rebellion at first; it looked like confidence.

He kept saying yes where God had already said "no." Not once. Not accidentally. But repeatedly. Each time, nothing seemed to happen. He still won battles. He still looked strong. He still functioned.

And therein lies the danger. Delayed consequences can trick us into thinking we're fine. Samson mistook survival for approval. He assumed strength meant immunity. But Scripture gives us a chilling line after Delilah cut his hair: "He did not know that the Lord had left him" (Judges 16:20).

Samson didn't lose his strength all at once. He lost belief first. He stopped believing he needed God to protect what God had given him.

Even then, grace was not gone. When Samson finally humbled himself, God restored his strength. The consequences remained, but redemption still had the final word.

Disbelief had a cost, but grace still met him there.

When Trauma Breaks the Agreement

I know this truth not just from Scripture but from my own life.

At nineteen years old, I was sexually assaulted. What that kind of trauma does isn't always obvious from the outside. It doesn't just hurt your body. It damages your sense of safety. It disrupts your trust—especially trust in boundaries.

Before the assault I had pledged to save myself for marriage and believed that "no" protected me. It had before. But after the assault, my belief fractured.

Something sacred was taken from me despite my refusal. Despite my boundaries. Despite my voice. And when that happens, your brain and body learn a dangerous lesson: "No" doesn't keep you safe.

Essentially, my trauma rewired my belief.

Trauma said to me that boundaries fail. It told me that control is safer than trust. It whispered, "agreeing might hurt less than resisting." And so afterward, I said yes to someone else. Someone I believed was safe and within my sphere of control—not because I wanted to, but because belief had been shaken.

I didn't fail because I lacked willpower. I failed because I stopped believing God's boundaries could still protect me.

After that, shame moved in quietly.

Shame doesn't shout. It whispers. It tells you that because you failed once, you've lost the right to speak again. That because your "no" didn't work before, it won't matter now.

For years, my voice froze in different types of moments when it should have been strong. It failed not because I was weak, but because shame convinced me I no longer had authority.

But that was never God's voice.

Scripture is clear that "there is now no condemnation for those who are in Christ Jesus" (Romans 8:1).

Meaning that trauma didn't cancel my calling. My failure to believe that my "no" mattered didn't erase authority, and my disbelief didn't disqualify me from repentance.

God does not withdraw when belief wavers. He restores it.

Faith After Pain

Please hear me loud and clear because what I learned post-trauma is that faith after pain does not mean you need to pretend you weren't hurt. It means we learn—slowly, gently—that God's "no" still protects, even when the world doesn't.

Some of the most painful moments of our lives aren't marked by what we did but by what we didn't stop.

But God is not finished with us just because our faith wavered.

So, what does faith look like after trauma? Faith is believing that God's "no" is still good. Faith is trusting that obedience still heals, even when it still hurts. And faith is choosing alignment, even after misalignment.

Just remember, God does not rush restoration. He rebuilds belief first.

R E F L E C T I O N

What happens when pain rewrites the story you believe about God? Take a moment to sit with that honestly. Has there been a season—perhaps one you have never fully named—when what happened to you made it harder for you to trust what God said? When His word felt distant, conditional, or even unsafe? You don't have to defend or dismiss that experience. But you do have to name it, because until we identify what broke our trust, we cannot begin to rebuild it. What specific experience, loss, or betrayal is still quietly shaping how much you trust God's voice today?

Consider where belief and obedience may have come apart in your own life. You may believe that God is good in a general sense while still struggling to trust that He is good specifically to you—in your body, your timing, your situation, the places where you have been most disappointed. Where does belief feel solid, and where does it feel fragile? Is there a specific area—a relationship, a loss, a prayer that went unanswered—where you have been waiting for God to explain Himself before you fully obey? What would it look like to take one step of obedience this week not after the explanation arrives but instead of it?

Father, I confess that there are places where pain has been louder than Your promise. Where experience has challenged what I say I believe, and where loss has made it hard to trust that Your "no" is still good—that it is still working for me even when it has cost me something I wanted deeply.

Heal the places where belief broke. Not just the surface places but the deep ones—where a violation, a loss, or a silence rewrote what I believed was true about Your character. I do not ask You to erase what happened. I ask You to redeem what it taught me about You.

Restore my trust in Your goodness—not as a vague concept but as a personal conviction. Help me believe not only that You are good in general, but also that You are good specifically to me, in my story, in the chapters I have not yet been able to explain. Give me the courage to say "no" when obedience draws me closer to You, and the healing that makes saying it possible.

In Jesus' mighty name, amen.

My Reflections

Personal notes from Chapter Two

CHAPTER THREE

When Yes Becomes a Hiding Place

For a long time I believed my inability to slow down was a strength.

I was dependable. Efficient. Always available. Always producing. Employers loved it, leaders praised it, and opportunities kept coming. From the outside, it looked like success. From the inside, it looked like a calendar with no white space and a woman who couldn't remember the last time she sat still without feeling restless—or guilty.

I wore busyness like a badge of honor. And to be fair, it worked. I got things done. I didn't procrastinate. I didn't need reminders. If something needed to be handled, I handled it quickly and thoroughly.

My life in that season—six children, a marriage, a career, and a calling—required more than a calendar could hold. People would look at me and say, "I don't know how you do it."

Well, frankly, neither did I.

When Busyness Is a Hiding Place

What I eventually learned through therapy and some very uncomfortable honesty was that my workaholism wasn't just ambition. It was a trauma response.

I began therapy to address multiple PTSD events in my life, which included PTSD from a military injury that carried its own physical and emotional weight. Somewhere in those conversations something finally clicked.

I wasn't always busy because I was driven. I was busy because stillness felt dangerous. How many of you can relate to that feeling? Not intentionally running from something but running just the same.

If we are always reacting, we are rarely discerning. If we are always saying yes, we may never pause long enough to hear what God is actually asking.

Silence and rest had become enemies. If I stopped moving, my thoughts might catch up with me. If my thoughts caught up, memories might surface. And if memories surfaced, feelings would follow. And who has time for feelings? Certainly not a woman who on the outside has it all, right? So I stayed busy.

Busyness gave me structure. It gave me validation. It gave me distance from pain. And the world rewarded it. In many professional and faith spaces, being constantly available is celebrated; productivity is praised and exhaustion is normalized.

But no one stopped to ask what it was costing me. And for a long time neither did I. I avoided it because I didn't see a problem.

Here is something we rarely talk about in faith spaces, but we need to: Sometimes our endless yeses are not obedience, they are avoidance.

Avoidance of pain. Avoidance of grief. Avoidance of healing. Avoidance of God's invitation to rest.

When the prophet Elijah was exhausted and afraid, God did not meet him in the wind, the earthquake, or the fire. God met him in a whisper (1 Kings 19:11–13). And you cannot hear a whisper if you never stop moving. I know I couldn't. I have wondered if in that season of busy I missed something God had for me because I was not still enough to hear from Him.

If we are always reacting, we are rarely discerning. If we are always saying yes, we may never pause long enough to ask or hear what God is actually saying.

Running from the Assignment

Jonah understood this dynamic better than most—not at first though.

God's instruction to Jonah was clear: Go to Nineveh. Jonah did not misunderstand the assignment nor did he need clarification. He simply did not want to obey it. So he did what many of us do when we "don't have time for that." He went in the opposite direction.

If we're honest, Jonah reads like a case study in spiritual oppositional defiance. God said go east; Jonah booked passage west. God called him to confront him; Jonah chose escape. God invited obedience; Jonah chose to run. How many of us are running from God because we don't have the time, energy, capacity, or desire to do another "thing"?

And here's the uncomfortable truth: Jonah wasn't hiding in laziness. He was hiding in busyness. And busyness feels productive; doesn't it?

But busyness can look like faithfulness when it is really resistance. And when we fill our lives with motion—opportunities, obligations, commitments—we often drown out the very voice trying to redirect us.

Some of us don't struggle to hear God. We struggle to surrender to what He says.

During a season when I was still carrying deep, unhealed trauma, I found myself desperate for healing—physical, emotional, and spiritual. My body was unraveling. My throat kept closing. I had just broken my finger. I was exhausted and afraid.

A coworker invited me to church, and it was my first time there.

As the service ended, I felt a clear, unmistakable prompting to get on my knees at the altar in front of me. I heard God plainly. And because I had a tendency to argue with God when I was young and immature, I refused. Have you ever done that? Tried to rationalize with God? Well I did, and it didn't go my way.

In that moment, I didn't want to be seen. I didn't want to be exposed. I didn't want to surrender that publicly. If I am being honest, I don't even know if I wanted God to see me like that. So, I stayed standing—stubborn, embarrassed, murmuring internally.

What I did not know at the time was that I was refusing my blessing.

God was ready to heal me in that moment, and I said "no"—not because I didn't hear Him but because I didn't want to obey Him that way.

Eventually, my knees buckled. I ended up in the very position I had resisted.

The lesson stayed with me: We can hear God clearly and still do the opposite of what He is telling us to do—not out of ignorance but out of fear, pride, discomfort, or resistance.

Jonah ran because he didn't want to confront what God was calling him to face. I stayed busy because I didn't want to sit with what God was calling me to do to heal.

Different routes. Same avoidance.

When we say yes to everything except rest, when we stay in motion instead of obedience, when our own voice becomes louder than God's, discernment dissipates. And without God's voice, we confuse desire with direction and mistake activity for ordained purpose.

God's Interruption as Mercy

Thank God for His grace and mercy.

The mercy in my story, and Jonah's, is that God did not withdraw His presence because of resistance. He stayed. He waited. And when necessary, He intervened—not to shame but to heal.

Jonah's storm was not rejection, and the fish was not abandonment.

Both were mercy. God used interruption to restore alignment.

When we hide in busyness, God invites stillness. When we drown out His voice with noise, God creates quiet. When we resist obedience because it feels costly or uncomfortable, God remains patient; He is firm but faithful.

Resistance may delay obedience, but it does not cancel calling.

What Rest Actually Requires

Therapy helped me name what faith alone hadn't healed. And faith helped me surrender what therapy alone couldn't carry.

I had to relearn truths I thought I already knew but failed to give in to. I learned that rest is not laziness and that stillness is not danger and that silence is not abandonment.

Jesus Himself withdrew often—not because He was weak but because He was aligned.

When I finally began saying "no"—not defensively but faithfully—space opened. I had space to breathe, space to heal, space to listen, and space to rest.

And in that space, God met me not with condemnation but with clarity. I didn't stop being capable, and I didn't stop being effective. I simply stopped being reactive.

And when reactivity gave way to rootedness, my yeses became intentional instead of compulsive. My "nos" became protective instead of defensive. And God was no longer squeezed into the margins of my schedule. In fact, I was more productive because I wasn't overextended, worried, or stressed.

God was once again at the center, right where He belongs.

Busyness is one of the most socially acceptable ways to stay numb. Before you move forward, take an honest inventory. What has your pace of yes been protecting you from? What has it been helping you avoid? Is it grief that hasn't been fully processed? A relationship that needs a hard conversation you keep postponing? A calling you haven't pursued because answering it would cost you the comfortable identity you have built around being the one who keeps everything running?

Think about the last time you genuinely felt at rest, not just physically still but spiritually settled. When was it? What made it possible? And what specific thing, one actual commitment, habit, or obligation would have to change for that kind of quiet to become more regular in your life? Whose approval are you still working to earn with your pace? Whose voice is behind the urgency that keeps you moving before you have finished listening? Name the person or the standard. And then ask: Is that standard God's, or did I inherit it from somewhere else entirely?

Lord, teach me to rest without fear. I confess that I have confused motion with obedience and busyness with faithfulness. I have filled my schedule in ways that left no room for You to speak and called that dedication. I have avoided stillness because stillness asks questions I have not wanted to answer.

Heal what my hurry has been hiding. Surface what my motion has been suppressing. And give me the courage to sit still long enough to hear what You have been waiting to say. Where my yeses have been driven by avoidance, redirect them. Where my pace has been driven by fear, slow me down.

Give me the courage to say "no" to what fills the time You want from me. And in the space that opens, meet me—not with condemnation but with clarity. Help me trust that rest is not laziness. That stillness is not stagnation. That the quiet You are calling me into is not empty; it is full of You.

In Jesus' mighty name, amen.

My Reflections

Personal notes from Chapter Three

CHAPTER FOUR

The Emotional and Spiritual Challenge of Saying No

By now, we understand that saying "no" is not simply a matter of confidence or discipline. If it were, most of us would have mastered it long ago and moved on with our lives.

If chapter 3 examined how we hide in yes, this chapter confronts a deeper and more unsettling question: Why does "no" feel unsafe even when we know better?

Awareness alone does not dissolve fear. Healing does not automatically restore authority. For many of us, the struggle to say "no" is not about discipline or confidence. It is about what our bodies and spirits learned when "no" was ignored, violated, or made to feel dangerous. It's also about the physical and spiritual weight that comes with refusal.

As we've already seen, awareness does not automatically make obedience easier. And knowing why we struggle does not automatically make saying "no" easier. In fact, sometimes it makes it harder because now we realize what is at stake.

For some of us, "no" does not feel neutral. It feels dangerous. It feels personal. And it feels costly.

And often, that weight has a history.

When the Body Learns Fear

For some of us, the difficulty with "no" is not theoretical. It is learned.

In the last chapter, I shared the story about a time in my life when I said "no" clearly, repeatedly, and with conviction, and my "no" meant nothing. I shared how something I held sacred was taken from me despite my refusal, my boundaries, and my voice. Without anyone saying it out loud, my body and spirit absorbed a devastating message: Your "no" does not matter. The message went beyond spiritual consequences. It had physical ones as well.

When a "no" is ignored or violated, the impact reaches far beyond that moment. It conditions the heart. It trains the nervous system. It quietly teaches us that resistance is ineffective and compliance is safer.

I became a yes person, not because I wanted to be, but because my sense of authority had been stripped away.

*Trauma may distort authority, but it
does not revoke it.*

When a "no" is violated, the damage goes beyond the act itself. It convinces the soul that boundaries are optional and teaches the body to freeze instead of resist. Over time, this loss of agency shows up in subtle but powerful ways.

We say yes when we mean "no." We overextend. We stay silent, not because we lack strength, but because through pain we learned that saying "no" does not keep us safe.

And here is a truth that deserves to be stated plainly: What was taken from you was never authorized by God. And what God did not authorize, He does not affirm.

Trauma may distort authority, but it does not revoke it.

There is a distinction we rarely name: the difference between having authority violated and allowing it to remain taken.

The first is not a choice, and the second is rarely conscious.

When a "no" is ignored, especially in moments of vulnerability, the injury does not end when the moment passes. Authority is not destroyed; it is buried. It becomes layered under fear, shame, and the learned belief that resistance is futile.

This is where many of us live far longer than we realize.

When authority remains taken, we stop trusting our own discernment. We second-guess our God-given instincts that were designed to protect us. We hesitate before setting boundaries, even when danger rises in our spirit. We tolerate what God never authorized not because we agree with it but because our nervous system learned that saying "no" once didn't help.

But that is not weakness. That is survival. That is a human response.

Survival may be necessary for a season, but survival is not the same as freedom.

And this is where discernment becomes critical because it is impossible to trust your "no" if you were taught it never mattered.

This is why discernment must be chosen actively, repeatedly, and almost always against urgency.

That is why reclaiming authority and relearning discernment matters so deeply.

Take Tamar in 2 Samuel 13. Tamar's story forces us to confront one of the most painful realities in Scripture: Sometimes a "no" is spoken clearly and still is ignored.

Tamar does everything right. She speaks with clarity. She reasons with wisdom. She names the wrong plainly. Scripture records her refusal without ambiguity. There is no confusion about her consent. There is no uncertainty about her resistance.

And yet her "no" does not protect her.

What follows is just as devastating as the violation itself. Tamar is sent away, isolated, and silenced. Her brother urges her to keep quiet, to carry the burden privately so the system can remain intact. The message is unmistakable: Your voice is inconvenient.

If Tamar's story ended there, it would teach despair. But Scripture does something extraordinary; it preserves her "no" forever.

God does not erase her refusal. He does not rewrite the story to soften it. But He also does not blame her silence afterward.

Instead, He ensures that her voice—ignored by men—is recorded by heaven.

Here is what Tamar's story teaches us: When people ignore your "no," they may violate authority in the moment, but they do not own it. The danger is not that Tamar's "no" was violated. The danger is when we begin to live as though that violation permanently defines our authority.

If Tamar represents the trauma of a violated "no," Hagar represents something equally painful: never being given the authority to say "no" at all.

Hagar's body is used to fulfill someone else's promise. She is given no choice, no consent, and no protection. When the arrangement becomes uncomfortable, she is blamed. When she flees in desperation, she is pursued—not to be rescued but to be returned.

And God meets her.

Not Abraham. Not Sarah. God.

He calls her by name. He sees her affliction. He acknowledges her suffering. In doing so, He restores something no human authority ever granted her: recognition of her humanity and worth.

Hagar becomes the first person in Scripture to name God: "The God who sees me."

This matters deeply for anyone whose authority was never honored in the first place. God does not wait for permission to restore dignity. He does not require us to have had a voice before He gives us one. He sees us even when no one else does—and seeing in Scripture, is an act of restoration.

But here is the quiet risk: if we continue to live as though we are unseen, even after God has revealed Himself, we unknowingly agree with the lie that authority was never ours to begin with.

Many of us never connect these dots.

We wonder why we cannot stop working when we are exhausted. Why we keep saying yes even when our spirit feels uneasy. Why slowing down feels threatening instead of peaceful.

But patterns do not appear out of nowhere. They are survival strategies that once protected us but no longer serve us.

This is where grace—and maybe a smile—belongs. If your nervous system formed beliefs about God before your Bible study ever caught up, you're not failing. You're human.

Healing does not happen by yelling at ourselves to do better. It happens by telling the truth about what taught us to survive.

When Discernment Must Be Instinctual

For some seasons of my life, slowing down simply wasn't an option.

I've served in roles where decisions were expected immediately, where responsiveness was not just appreciated, it was required. In one position alone I was responsible for responding to more than eight thousand emails in a single month.

You read that right.

Eight. Thousand. Emails.

Every message carried urgency. Every sender expected expediency and clarity. And every response had the potential to ripple outward into policy, politics, people, or public consequences.

There was no quiet room. No extended prayer retreat before hitting reply. No luxury of sitting with a decision for days.

Discernment was still required.

That season taught me something important: Discernment is not always about time. Sometimes it is about training.

When life moves fast, discernment cannot rely solely on long pauses. It has to be embedded. It has to become instinctual—not reactive but anchored. And that kind of discernment is cultivated long before the moment of pressure arrives.

Most of our decisions—even in high-pressure environments—are not moral dilemmas. They are discernment moments. And discernment is not asking, "Do I have time to pray about this?" but "Have I built a life that listens?"

In those seasons I learned to distinguish between decisions and directions.

Not every email required spiritual wrestling. Nor did every request demand a theological debate. Many decisions were operational, procedural, or administrative.

Direction, however, required protection.

If a decision affected my integrity, my family, my values, or my long-term calling, it demanded attention—even when the timeline was tight. I learned to ask myself quickly but honestly: Does this align with who God has called me to be? If the answer was "no"—or unclear—I slowed that decision down.

I also learned the power of pre-decided boundaries.

When you know what you stand for and who you serve in advance, decisions don't need to be debated under pressure. I didn't need to discern whether I would compromise my integrity or sacrifice my family unnecessarily. Those answers were already clear.

Jesus modeled this. His responses in the wilderness were immediate not because He was rushed, but because He was anchored.

I learned to respect unease even when I couldn't fully explain it. Scripture tells us that the peace of God guards our hearts and minds. That guarding does not always come with explanation; it often comes as restraint.

And I learned that not every decision requires explanation.

Clarity is efficient. And let's face it; justification is exhausting.

Nehemiah understood this when he said, "I am carrying on a great project and cannot go down" (Nehemiah 6:3). That was it and that was all. He did not write a memo on the reasons he needed to stay where he was. He was matter of fact and to the point.

So how does one gain that confidence in a hurried season?

I am sure you have heard people say that the word Bible stands for Basic Instructions Before Leaving Earth, right? Well in seasons where everything moved quickly for me, I leaned heavily on Scripture as my guide because it has everything I need to help me through whatever season I am in. The Scripture that guides my work is Luke 4:18. If I really use that Scripture as my guide to whether I should say yes to a project or opportunity, I will make the right decision every time.

If it doesn't pass the filter, I don't meditate on it—and I don't say yes to it.

Discernment is not only about decisions. It's about what we allow to occupy our mind because when we ruminate too long on things that don't pass the sniff test, we tend to change our mind and choose the wrong path.

Reclaiming Authority Through Truth

So how do we reclaim authority?

We don't do it by forcing ourselves to be louder. Or by shaming ourselves for freezing. Or by pretending the pain didn't happen.

We reclaim it by believing what God says is true—even when experience taught us otherwise.

"I have given you authority to trample on snakes and scorpions and to overcome all the power of the enemy; nothing will harm you" (Luke 10:19).

"Submit yourselves, then, to God. Resist the devil, and he will flee from you" (James 4:7).

"There is now no condemnation for those who are in Christ Jesus" (Romans 8:1).

Again, authority is not erased by trauma. It is restored by truth.

So here's the bottom line up front: When we stop equating "no" with danger, rejection, or futility, something shifts. Our "no" doesn't need permission from people to be valid anymore. It only needs agrement with God. "It is for freedom that Christ has set us free. Stand firm, then, and do not let yourselves be burdened again by a yoke of slavery" (Galatians 5:1).

Freedom does not mean we are never challenged again. It just means we no longer surrender our authority when we are.

REFLECTION

Before you move forward, take an honest moment with this question: Where did you first learn that your "no" was not safe? Not in an abstract sense but specifically, in your body, in your history. Was it the time a boundary you tried to set was overridden? The moment when speaking up led to punishment or rejection? The relationship where your refusal was treated as betrayal? We carry these experiences not just as memories but as reflexes, as the way our chest tightens before we speak, as the hesitation that comes before the word "no" even forms. What is your "no" still protecting you from? And is that protection serving you now or keeping you from something God is calling you to claim?

Now consider what lie that experience planted in you. Not what you know theologically, but what you actually believe in practice—in the middle of a tense conversation when someone leans on you with expectation in their eyes, when you feel yourself beginning to fold before you have even finished forming a thought. What does your body believe your "no" will cost you? Name it without judgment. Then consider this: Think of one specific person in your life right now whose reaction to your "no" you are most afraid of. What are you afraid they will do, withdraw, retaliate, leave, or simply be disappointed? How many of your last ten decisions have been quietly shaped by managing that fear? What would it look like to make one decision this week based on what God says instead of what that person might feel?

PRAYER

Lord, restore what was taken from me. Heal the places where my voice was ignored, where my boundary was violated, where my "no" was used against me or treated as though it had no weight. I bring those moments to You now—not to rehearse them but to release what they taught me about my own worth.

Help me believe Your truth about who I am—that I am not without authority, not without worth, not without the right to say "no." Where trauma rewrote what I believe about my voice, speak louder. Where shame settled into patterns I still carry, name them by their true source—not by mine.

Teach me to say "no" from a place of peace, not panic. Not from the wounded place that has been taught silence, but from the healed place that has relearned strength. I am not the person I was in those moments that taught me to go quiet. I am becoming someone new. Walk with me into that becoming.

In Jesus' mighty name, amen.

My Reflections

Personal notes from Chapter Four

CHAPTER FIVE

The Power Dynamics of Yes and No

After authority is restored internally, a new challenge inevitably emerges: The world does not always welcome your boundaries.

Even when we have healed enough to say "no" with peace, we often discover that refusal still disrupts expectations, systems, and relationships. That's because yes and "no" are never neutral words. They carry power—socially, emotionally, and spiritually. And when that power shifts, resistance often follows.

Sometimes the resistance is obvious. Other times, it is subtle, wrapped in disappointment, confusion, or spiritual language that makes us question ourselves. But one truth becomes unavoidable as we mature in discernment: Obedience does not guarantee approval.

In everyday conversation, yes and "no" appear simple—short responses, efficient, and maybe even harmless. But in practice, they communicate far more than agreement or refusal. Both yes and "no" are complete sentences in and of themselves.

A yes can reinforce a system. A "no" can expose it. A yes can preserve comfort. A "no" can challenge dependency. And when people have grown accustomed to your availability, your refusal may feel personal even when it isn't.

Culture has long painted "no" as the uncooperative answer, the word of the difficult person, the ungrateful employee, the uncommitted member. Yes, on the other hand, is framed as generosity, flexibility, and commitment. The person who always says yes is praised as dependable. The one who says "no" is often labeled difficult. But perception is not reality. Clear boundaries build trust, respect, and sustainability. Saying "no" with conviction is not rejection; it is honesty. It is truth-telling about capacity, priority, and calling.

The problem is that truth-telling is disruptive especially in workplaces, families, and even faith spaces that rely on constant availability.

When Obedience Disrupts Expectations

I learned this the hard way.

There was a season in my life when everything I was doing looked spiritual, productive, and right—at least from the outside. We were living in Illinois. I had three of my six children at the time, all under the age of five. I was working full-time, managing a household, and was deeply involved in church. Bible study meant forty-minute drives each way. Ministry involvement meant late nights, full calendars, and a steady stream of "Sure, I can help with that."

I said yes because I believed I was serving God.

Meanwhile, at home, something was unraveling. My husband grew frustrated—not because he opposed my faith, but because I was rarely present. Our children needed me. My marriage needed me. And I felt torn, defensive, and guilty all at once. How could something that felt so holy be creating so much strain?

I believed my yeses were obedience, but God was trying to show me they were in fact imbalance.

Generosity Without Discernment

That same tension showed up in another area of my life: generosity.

When we lived in Illinois, I had a neighbor who asked for help constantly. Sugar. Flour. Household items. Blankets. And for a long time, we gave freely. We were also trying to invite her and her children to church because I wanted her to get to know the God I serve. And while we didn't have much, we wanted to live out our faith generously and tangibly. Giving felt like the right thing to do.

Then one day, I told her "no" because God told me to tell her "no." And it was one of those "noes" I couldn't understand at the time.

Her response to my "no" caught me off guard. She became angry and said, "But you're supposed to be a Christian."

In that moment, a light bulb turned on. I saw clear as day that some people will use your kindness as leverage. And some will try to use the God in you against you. Her words didn't shame me; they clarified me. They confirmed what I already knew in my spirit. This "no" was right.

Not long after that, she stopped coming around.

The lesson stayed with me: Obedience will not always be rewarded with gratitude. Sometimes it is rewarded with God-ordained distance.

Generosity is a gift of the Spirit. Scripture affirms that plainly. But generosity without discernment becomes compulsion. And compulsion—especially spiritualized compulsion—will quietly erode peace, unity, and stewardship.

There were times my husband and I argued because I felt pressured to help family and friends, even when it created tension at home. But when I began praying first—really praying—and coming into agreement with my spouse, the answers became clearer. Sometimes the answer was yes. Sometimes it was "no." And sometimes it was yes, but differently.

And what changed was not my heart, it was my posture.

I stopped confusing generosity with obligation.

This shift reframed everything. If everything I have belongs to God, why would I give it away without consulting Him? We would never want someone else giving away our belongings without our permission no matter how noble the cause. But how often do we do exactly that with God's resources?

Scripture tells us that "the earth is the Lord's, and everything in it" (Psalm 24:1).

We are stewards, not owners, of everything that belongs to Him. And stewardship requires us to seek Him in all that we do.

Clarity Does Not Require Justification

This truth eventually reached beyond generosity and into leadership, calling, and opportunity.

When I was presented with an opportunity to work in Washington, DC, I knew the answer was "no" before I ever said it out loud. I had prayed. I had wrestled. I had listened. The decision itself was clear. What wasn't clear was how to deliver it.

I didn't want to disappoint the people who extended the invitation. I didn't want to seem ungrateful, fearful, or incapable. So instead of letting my "no" stand, I tried to soften it with an explanation. I justified it. I contextualized it. I gave reasons that were true but unnecessary.

When the conversation ended, I didn't feel peace. I felt exposed. And then I ruminated for weeks.

That experience taught me something I now live by in every area of my life: Clarity does not require justification.

Remember Nehemiah? He understood this.

Scripture tells us that when Nehemiah was rebuilding the wall, his enemies did not attack him with weapons at first. They attacked him with distraction. They asked him to come down from the work for a meeting. Just a conversation. Just an explanation. Nehemiah's response was unwavering: "I am carrying on a great project and cannot go down" (Nehemiah 6:3). He did not insult them. He did not explain himself. He did not manage their disappointment. He simply refused.

And when they asked again, he gave the same answer.

Nehemiah teaches us something critical: When people cannot move you off your obedience, they will try to move you into explanation.

Nehemiah resisted, and Jesus modeled this restraint even more profoundly.

After delivering a difficult teaching about eating his flesh and drinking his blood (John 6:51–58), many of His disciples walked away. These were not enemies. These were followers. And Jesus did not chase them, nor did He soften the truth or explain Himself. Instead, He turned to the twelve and asked, "You do not want to leave too, do you?" (John 6:67).

That was not indifference. That was authority rooted in love.

Being Christlike does not mean preventing disappointment. God Himself was not apologetic about the consequences Adam and Eve faced. He did not explain His timing to Abraham. He did not justify discipline to David, and He never loved them less.

Love can be clear. Love can be firm. And
love can allow disappointment to exist
without rescuing people from it.

This matters deeply for believers who equate kindness with emotional management.

Love can be clear. Love can be firm. And love can allow disappointment to exist without rescuing people from it.

Moses lived this tension daily. The people murmured, complained, and resisted—even after deliverance. Moses did not negotiate with them over God's commands. He spoke what God said and allowed the people to wrestle with it.

Whether in ministry, family, or vocation leadership requires the courage to let others sit with a "no" they do not like.

If someone you love struggles with your refusal, the Christlike response is not to overexplain. It is to remain anchored. You can acknowledge your feelings without reopening doors. You can listen without surrendering boundaries. You can love without absorbing responsibility for others' reactions.

Sometimes, the most faithful thing you can do is say less. I believe in that so much that it should go on a t-shirt: Say less!

*When God Removes You Before You
Remove Yourself*

Sometimes when we refuse to say "no," God intervenes.

During that same season of overcommitment at church, I was placed on military orders and ultimately gone from my family for nearly a year. I never deployed overseas, but I was severely injured. Everything stopped. And the busyness? It disappeared—not because I chose rest, but because it became irrelevant.

God had been nudging me to step back long before He removed me. I just hadn't listened.

Looking back, I can see that a timely "no"—earlier, quieter, chosen—may have spared me pain. Instead, a severe injury ushered in a dark season of my life, one where I no longer felt purposeful or useful. I truly felt like I was in the wilderness. I went from constant busyness to forced stillness in the most unimaginable way, and sitting in that stillness was unbearable.

It felt like whiplash. I wondered if I would ever have a sense of purpose again.

But even when my faith wavered, God remained faithful. He used interruption to restore alignment. He used stillness to bring clarity. And He used that season to mold me, raising me from the ashes like a phoenix, not in spite of the pause but because of it.

God often invites us to stop long before He requires us to. Our only responsibility is to assume the right posture, to listen, to trust, and to respond.

REFLECTION

Think about a season when someone responded to your "no" with resistance, whether overt or subtle. Maybe they repeated the ask. Maybe they pulled back. Maybe they questioned your commitment, your faith, or your character. And maybe, if you are honest, their reaction worked. You came back. You overexplained. You eventually said yes because the cost of holding the line felt greater than the cost of releasing it. What happened inside you in that moment? What did you feel? What did you tell yourself you had to become for others to stay?

Now consider where that pattern shows up today. Are there specific relationships or roles where your "no" has never quite landed with full authority, where you are still waiting for someone to approve it before it feels final? Who specifically holds the power to undo your convictions simply by expressing disappointment? Name that person not to blame them but to bring clarity. As long as someone else's emotion holds more authority over your decisions than God's voice does, you are living under their leadership not His. What would it look like to have one conversation this week with that specific person where you hold your "no" without apologizing for it, without overexplaining it, and without going back on it? You don't have to be harsh. You just have to be clear. What would you need to believe about God's faithfulness to actually do that?

PRAYER

Father, teach me to say yes with intention and "no" with conviction. Free me from the belief that I must be available to prove my worth. Free me from the exhaustion of managing other people's reactions to my obedience as though their comfort is my responsibility, and their approval is my calling.

Show me where the power dynamics around me have been shaping my decisions more than Your voice has. And give me the discernment to recognize the difference between manipulation and genuine need, between someone who wants my compliance and someone who needs my care.

Help me root my decisions not in what people expect but in what You commission, not in urgency but in obedience. And where my "no" disrupts systems that were built on my silence, give me the courage to let them be disrupted, trusting that You are able to hold what I release.

In Jesus' mighty name, amen.

My Reflections

Personal notes from Chapter Five

CHAPTER SIX

Learning to Hear Before We Decide

One of the most honest confessions I can make is this:

I don't always know if I'm hearing from God or from the little voice in my head.

There. I said it.

That admission alone will unsettle some people, especially in faith spaces where confidence is often mistaken for clarity and decisiveness is confused with discernment. Because of my controlling tendencies, I—like many of you—prefer my spiritual decisions to be clean, fast, and stamped with certainty from God. Essentially, we want God's voice to be unmistakable, authoritative, and preferably loud enough to drown out every competing thought.

But for many of us, that is not how God actually works.

The Problem of Noise

More often than not, our struggle isn't rebellion. It's noise. Loud, messy, distracting noise.

So before we can talk about saying yes or "no" with confidence, we have to talk about learning how to listen at all.

Here is the truth: We live in a hurried world, rushed culture, a society that prizes immediacy and rewards speed. We want our food done fast, our promotions to come sooner, our sermons to be twenty minutes or less, and our money to move just as quickly. Decisions are expected instantly. Responses are demanded immediately. Silence is uncomfortable, and waiting is often interpreted as weakness or indecision.

And that posture doesn't stop when we enter faith spaces.

We rush prayer, we skim Scripture, and we want answers before we've sat long enough to hear instruction.

And when we don't hear God clearly, we often don't stop; we substitute. We lean on logic. We lean on precedent. We lean on other people's expectations. And sometimes, we lean on fear, fear of being wrong, fear of missing out, fear of disappointing someone, and fear of closing a door that might never open again.

I know this fear well. I am a recovering perfectionist. Perfectionism has always lived close to my decision-making. I want to get it right, and I want to honor God in the process. I also want to be obedient. But I don't want to miss an opportunity that feels important or irreversible.

So sometimes, instead of waiting to hear clearly, I rush to decide, and I deviate from God's plan. And I've learned the hard way that rushing does not produce peace; it produces justification, chaos, and confusion.

So here's a question many of us are afraid to ask out loud: How do I know the difference between God's voice and my own?

Let's be honest. Our thoughts can sound very convincing, especially when they're dressed up in spiritual language.

"I feel led" can sometimes mean "I really want this." "I have peace" can sometimes mean "I'm relieved I decided." "This door opened" can sometimes mean "This option didn't say 'no.'" I know you know this, but not every internal nudge is divine instruction, and not every open door is God's invitation.

Scripture tells us that God is not the author of confusion and that clarity often comes slowly not suddenly. Ugh, for someone who moves fast, that is not what I wanted to hear. But here's the thing, discernment is rarely dramatic. It is usually quiet, cumulative, and confirmed over time. That's why learning to hear God requires posture before it requires action.

Throughout Scripture, the people who heard God most clearly were rarely the ones in a hurry. In fact, Moses encountered God in a wilderness he hadn't planned to be in. Samuel heard God's voice while lying still, not while striving. Elijah discovered that God was not in the wind, the earthquake, or the fire but in a whisper.

Remember, a whisper requires proximity, and proximity requires stillness.

We cannot hear God clearly when our own desires are shouting over Him. And we cannot discern His voice when we are unwilling to slow down long enough to test what we think we've heard. But here's the uncomfortable truth: Many of us are not too busy to hear God; we are too distracted.

We say we don't have time, but what we often mean is that we haven't prioritized stillness. And sometimes, if we're being honest, that avoidance has a name: spiritual laziness.

It's not irreverence or rebellion. It's just a subtle resistance to the work of slowing down, listening, and waiting when answers aren't immediate.

When God Is Silent

One of the hardest moments in discernment is silence because when God is silent that silence feels very loud.

When God does not answer immediately, we think maybe He didn't hear us, so we ask again. When prayer feels one sided, we begin to feel like He doesn't care. And when Scripture doesn't leap off the page with clarity, we begin to question whether we are mature Christians.

Have you ever sat through a speech—or given one—where there was a pause between words that felt uncomfortable? We sometimes call it a dramatic pause. You can see people looking around. Maybe they start to squirm in their chairs. Maybe they feel anxious for the speaker. The pause feels like an eternity, even though it might only be ten seconds. Try it sometime as a social experiment and watch the room. If you're not sure what I mean right now, you will after you do it.

That uneasy feeling is the same feeling many of us experience when God is silent. We tend to panic.

Silence, in general, makes us anxious. It triggers our need to resolve uncertainty. We want answers. We want clarity. We want movement. And if we are not careful, we will rush to fill that silence with our own reasoning and then call it faith.

But filling the silence is not the same as trusting God in it.

When God is quiet, our temptation is not just to wait less; it is to take control more. We start connecting our own dots, creating our own explanations, and making our own plans. And before we realize it, we are no longer listening for God's direction.

We are simply moving because the silence feels too uncomfortable to sit in.

Take Abraham and Sarah. God promised them a son, and because they were waiting so long and were old, they decided to take matters into their own hands and conceive a child by other means. And that decision ultimately led to unnecessary chaos and drama.

Scripture never treats God's silence as absence. Often, silence is an invitation to wait, to trust, to discern, and to examine one's motives.

I cannot recall a single time God explained to me why He said "no" or why He said nothing. I had to live long enough to understand it. And there are still things for which I haven't heard from Him.

God is not obligated to justify His boundaries to us. He does not owe us an explanation before obedience, and He never withholds love simply because He withholds information. In the case of Abraham and Sarah, God still blessed them with the son He promised them despite their decision to take matters into their own hands.

Discerning Your Voice from His

But our own thoughts aren't the only thoughts we have to contend with. Other people, people we love and respect, can sometimes cloud God's yeses and "noes" for us as well.

This became especially real for me when my son was nearly three years old and diagnosed with autism.

The news itself was heavy. Not because I believed something was wrong with my child but because I knew the world would not always be kind to him. I also knew what the diagnosis meant. It opened a door to early intervention services, support, and resources that could help him thrive.

But almost immediately, the voices started.

Some people close to me—people I loved—urged me not to accept the diagnosis. They reminded me that Black children are often mislabeled. They warned me about the stigma. Others, particularly in church spaces, told me I shouldn't "claim it." That Jesus could heal him, so I should reject the diagnosis outright, which would essentially close the door to intervention.

And here's what made it complicated: None of that advice sounded evil. Much of it sounded loving. And some of it even sounded faithful.

But it wasn't God's voice.

In that season, I had to learn again that discernment cannot be outsourced. Even to people who love us. Even to people who quote Scripture.

I believed God could heal my son. I still do. But I also believed God was sending help through the early intervention services. So I said yes to the diagnosis, to the resources, to the therapists who came into my home, to early schooling, and to special services.

And I trusted God to meet us there.

Before long, my son began speaking. He no longer needed sign language. He learned how to find his way in the world more independently. Healing and provision did not compete; they collaborated. And today he is acting in plays and writing songs. He is who God created him to be.

That experience taught me something I will never forget: Faith does not mean denying reality. Faith means listening closely enough to recognize how God is moving. And that kind of listening requires relationship.

So how do I figure out if it is God or me? When I'm unsure whether I'm hearing God or myself I take my rationale to Scripture. I don't look for loopholes or cherry-pick verses for confirmation. Instead I test the alignment.

I ask questions like "Does this decision reflect God's character?" "Does it produce peace not pressure?" "Does it require deception, overexplaining, or self-justification?" "Does it honor my responsibilities not just my desires?" And here's a humbling confession: sometimes I already know the answer, but I don't like it.

Sometimes God's direction is clear, but it's inconvenient. Sometimes His "no" interrupts our momentum. Sometimes His silence forces us to have patience. That's usually when I realize the tension isn't discernment; it's the dreaded word surrender.

The Work of Surrender

In order for us to fully hear from God, we must surrender. And I know personally that surrender is hard when you are a perfectionist, a control freak, or both!

And we all know that there is a particular kind of anxiety that lives between perfectionism and urgency. I don't want to make the wrong decision. But I also don't want to miss the right one.

That tension has caused me to rush when I should have waited and to wait when I should have moved. It has caused me to overthink, overpray, and overexplain decisions that simply needed to be obeyed. Faith does not require flawless decision-making. It requires a faithful posture.

God is not surprised by our humanity. I know He is definitely not surprised by mine. He is not undone by our uncertainty either. And He is not waiting to punish us for imperfect discernment. But He does invite us to seek Him and listen before we leap.

Another way I've grown in this area is learning to say less. More people should choose this practice as the default. Imagine a world where people didn't say every little thing that came to mind, especially online while hiding behind a computer screen. We would surely have more peace, more marriages would survive, and our mouths wouldn't be so exhausted.

I used to explain my "no," justify my pause, and even narrate my discernment process aloud, in emails, to supervisors, you name it.

I didn't do that because it was necessary, but because I wanted people to understand. I didn't want to disappoint them, and I didn't want to seem ungrateful or unfaithful.

And afterward, I would replay every word in my head, wondering if I'd said too much, explained too much, or revealed too much.

Constant rumination became the price of overexplaining. What I've learned since is that clarity does not require commentary. Period.

Did Jesus explain every "no?" Nope. Does God defend every boundary? No. And aren't we called to model after Jesus? Well, one way to do that is to say less.

Learning to hear God also means learning when not to speak prematurely.

When we trust God's response, we don't have to say much or explain ourselves. The outcome will speak for itself.

The truth is, many of our struggles with saying yes or "no" are not about boundaries; they're about trust.

Do we trust God enough to wait? Do we trust God's response? Do we trust Him enough to disappoint people? Do we trust Him enough to be misunderstood for a season?

Because sometimes, obedience looks like delay. Sometimes it looks like restraint. And sometimes it looks like sitting still when every instinct tells you to move.

Learning to hear God before deciding doesn't eliminate uncertainty, but it anchors us in relationship rather than reaction. And when we finally do move, when the yes or "no" becomes clear, it carries a different weight.

There is no panic or pressure—just peace and confidence.

And the confidence God offers is not loud. It is not hurried, and it does not require immediate validation.

It is the quiet assurance that says, I waited. I listened. And I moved when it was time.

And sometimes, that confidence comes only after we've learned to sit in the discomfort of not knowing without rushing to resolve it.

My friends, that is not weakness. That is maturity.

REFLECTION

Consider the last significant decision you made. How much time passed between the moment the opportunity arrived and the moment you answered? And in that window—however wide or narrow—did you genuinely listen, or did you perform the appearance of listening while already rehearsing what you would say? There is a difference between pausing and discerning. A pause is about timing. Discernment is about surrender. Before answering, did you actually give God space to speak, or did you simply wait long enough to feel sure you could justify whatever you had already decided?

Think about a time when you moved too quickly, when you answered from urgency, pressure, or enthusiasm before you had genuinely listened. What did that cost you, not just in outcome but in the quiet internal aftermath—the sense that you had missed something, or said yes before you were ready? And what does it look like practically for you to listen well before you decide—not in theory but in the actual shape of your week? Is there a practice—prayer, journaling, silence, seeking counsel—that you know helps you hear more clearly but you have not been consistent in doing? What specific decision are you facing right now that deserves that kind of attention before you answer?

Lord, teach me to listen before I decide. Help me to truly listen, not just sit in silence long enough to confirm what I have already resolved. Help me to be genuinely open, to hold the question loosely enough for You to answer it in ways I did not anticipate.

Quiet the noise of fear, perfectionism, and urgency that competes with Your voice. Remind me that You are not shouting over the chaos. You are speaking beneath it, to the part of me that only hears when I finally stop. Help me resist the cultural pressure to respond quickly and the spiritual pressure to appear decisive. Help me trust that a pause is not a failure.

When I am unsure, speak. When I am pressured, steady me. When I move ahead of You, bring me gently back—not with condemnation but with the quiet authority of a Father who knows where I am going better than I do. Teach me that clarity is a gift You give to those who are willing to wait for it.

In Jesus' mighty name, amen.

My Reflections

Personal notes from Chapter Six

CHAPTER SEVEN

When Obedience Costs Something

Life has a way of presenting crossroads at the exact moment we feel most ready—or most desperate—for a breakthrough.

Some opportunities arrive quietly, asking us to listen closely. Others arrive loudly, wrapped in prestige, affirmation, and just enough validation to make us assume they must be from God. These are the opportunities that feel like answered prayers—the kind that make you say, Surely, this is it.

But Scripture, and experience, teach us something far more nuanced: Not every open door is an assignment, and not every opportunity is God's timing.

So let's talk about those moments when saying yes feels faithful, logical, and earned, but obedience quietly asks us to wait. These are the moments that reveal whether we are led by excitement, fear of missing out, ambition, or discernment.

When the Door Looks Like Destiny

On three occasions, I was presented with prestigious career opportunities to work alongside the White House. On paper, they were everything I had worked toward and hoped for: recognition, advancement, influence. These open doors where the kind people pray for and then pretend they're not, hoping God hears them.

And twice I said no.

Each time, the internal struggle was intense. I prayed. I paced. I talked through it with trusted people. I wrestled with the same question many believers face: If God brought this open door to me, why does walking through it feel wrong?

I wanted to say yes. I really did. I also wanted to believe that trusting God meant walking through every door that looked divine. But something deeper was happening. My husband and I were not aligned. There was still work I had been called to complete in the role I was already in. And most importantly, I did not have peace.

At the same time these opportunities appeared, my marriage was fragile. We were in the beginning stages of healing, but we were nowhere near stable. We were rebuilding our relationship carefully and intentionally, but it was still in a tender stage.

Deep down I knew that stepping into a high-demand role hundreds of miles from home at that moment could fracture what we were still repairing. That realization forced an uncomfortable truth into the open: Sometimes callings compete—not because one is wrong, but because timing matters. It was obvious our marriage was still so fragile, but I strongly contemplated taking the risk anyway. Unfortunately, I was willing to do what I had done before therapy: run.

So how did I come to a crossroads where God ultimately had me choose between what I believed were two things worth fighting for? During the pandemic, my adult daughters and I held a goal-setting session. We wrote things down—dreams, prayers, intentions. Two priorities rose to the top with surprising clarity.

First, I wanted to work in a senior leadership role within the Department of Veterans Affairs one day. I had no idea how that would happen. I lived in a small town. I didn't know anyone inside the organization.

Second, it was important to me that my marriage would be strengthened and restored.

About a year later, the call came—from the White House—asking whether I was interested in a position within the administration. It felt surreal. How did they even get my name? I wondered. How would this work logistically? Surely this was God answering my prayers.

But something wasn't right. This great opportunity came at the same time my marriage was on the rocks.

The Test of the Premature Yes

Have you ever considered that some opportunities are not given to advance us but to test our resolve?

Scripture is filled with moments where God intentionally delays or redirects opportunity—not to punish but to prepare.

> *Sometimes the greatest test of faith isn't*
> *waiting for the promise. It's refusing to*
> *rush it.*

David knew something about that.

He was anointed king while Saul still sat on the throne. The calling was undeniable. The promise was spoken. The destiny was sealed, and yet years passed before the promise was realized.

More than once, David found himself with a clear opportunity to seize what God had already promised him. The most striking moment came when David found Saul vulnerable in the cave — and chose to walk away. From a human perspective, it looked like divine delivery.

But David said no. He refused to take what God had promised before God released it. He said, "The Lord forbid that I should do such a thing to my master, the Lord's anointed" (1 Samuel 24:6).

God was protecting David's heart from shortcuts. He was teaching him that destiny seized prematurely can become corruption. The delay preserved David's integrity—and ultimately his kingdom.

Sometimes the greatest test of faith isn't waiting for the promise. It's refusing to rush it.

During that season, I felt a little like Abraham standing on the mountain with Isaac, not because I believed God wanted to take something from me forever, but because I didn't know He was capable of giving it back.

Waiting felt costly. Waiting felt risky. Waiting felt like choosing faith without any assurance of outcome. Obedience required me to trust God without knowing there would be another call. But as Scripture says, "There is a time for everything, and a season for every activity under the heavens" (Ecclesiastes 3:1)

Obedience doesn't always feel peaceful at first. Sometimes it feels like loss.

Jesus understood this kind of restraint. After feeding the five thousand, the crowds were electrified. They wanted to make Him king . . . by force. The affirmation was overwhelming. The platform was ready. Influence, power, recognition—everything the world uses to measure success—was right in front of Him. Yet Jesus walked away. "Jesus, knowing that they intended to come and make Him king by force, withdrew again to a mountain by Himself" (John 6:15).

A crown without a cross would have short-circuited redemption. Saying no preserved the purpose of His life. Sometimes walking away from applause is obedience.

What God's "Not Yet" Is Protecting

That truth came alive for me in a way I didn't expect.

I knew that if I left my current role during that season and moved across the country, my marriage of twenty-three years likely would not survive. And for the first time in my life, I understood Abraham in a way I never had before.

Abraham prayed for a son. God gave him Isaac, the fulfillment of a lifelong promise. And then God asked Abraham to lay that promise on the altar. God presented me with an opportunity I had prayed for. One that I may have never gotten on my own. And then God asked me to choose between my marriage and the opportunity. He challenged me to lay one of them on the altar.

The test was not cruel, but it was to strengthen my obedience.

God had allowed me to taste the fulfillment of a professional prayer, but obedience required me to lay it down—not forever but for that season.

I chose my marriage, and I know I made the right decision. But if I'm honest, I didn't choose it gracefully at first.

I was frustrated. I was disappointed. I was quietly resentful. I blamed my husband for holding me back. After all, this wasn't just any opportunity. This was a chance to work for a President. A chance to serve at the highest levels of government.

Surely, if God brought this to me, agreement was supposed to follow, right?

In prayer, my heart wrestled hard. "Lord, You brought this to me. You placed this opportunity in front of me. And now You're asking me to lay it down?" And it happened twice!

It felt unfair. It felt costly. It felt like obedience without assurance of outcome.

I genuinely believed that by turning down two opportunities like that I had closed the door permanently. Opportunities at that level don't usually circle back.

But what prayer eventually revealed was this: God had not said yes yet. And He had not said leave. He still had work for me to do right where I was.

The Honest Confession

Something else surfaced. Something that was harder to admit.

I realized that my desire to say yes wasn't entirely selfless. Part of it was pride. Part of it was ambition. Part of it was wanting control. My habit of saying yes had sometimes been a form of self-indulgence not obedience.

That realization was painful and convicting but also freeing.

Almost eighteen months later, another opportunity came. It was with the same organization, but everything was different.

My marriage was stronger than ever before. We had gone to therapy. We prayed together. We built a business together. We were aligned.

The position itself felt uncanny, as if it had been written specifically for my skill set, my experience, and the work God had been quietly shaping in me all along. There was peace—not ease but peace.

This time, saying yes did not cost my marriage. It strengthened it.

I learned something I will never forget:

God's not yet is often an act of mercy. And His yes, when it comes, leaves no confusion behind.

What I did not fully anticipate when I finally said yes to the role was that saying yes did not end the decision-making. It intensified it. The pressure did not decrease once I was inside; it multiplied. I was no longer making decisions that affected a team or a region. I was making decisions at a national and international scale with stakeholders whose names I had only read in briefings. The wrong yes could have consequences I would not be able to walk back.

Discernment was not a luxury in that environment. It was a survival skill. There were moments when relying on it cost me something visible—an opportunity declined, a meeting missed, a connection not made—that I would later understand was protection I could not have engineered on my own.

One of those moments stands out clearly. An international organization extended an invitation to attend a conference their home country. Several of my colleagues said yes. I said no. I could not fully articulate why at the time—only that something in my spirit went quiet in a way I had learned to take seriously. The opportunity looked legitimate. The relationship looked professional. But something felt off.

Not long after, the story broke. The individual hosting that conference had been publicly branded a criminal and a scammer in his country. It was widely covered. Photographs of some of my colleagues who had attended began circulating online alongside his name. Photographs are permanent. The internet does not forget. And in a role where credibility is currency, those images carried weight that no explanation could fully undo.

I do not say this to diminish the colleagues who went. They made a reasonable decision with the information they had. But I know with clarity that what kept me from being in those photographs was not superior judgment or better research. It was the quiet no of the Holy Spirit, and my willingness to honor Him even when I could not explain it. When I strayed from that kind of discernment, I failed. Every time. Not occasionally. Every time.

But here is what I want you to hold: These moments are not reserved for people in high-profile roles. The same Spirit that steadied my decision in a government office is the same Spirit available to a fourteen-year-old working her first job at McDonald's.

I was that teenager. I remember the day clearly. Someone had unscrewed the bottoms of the salt and pepper shakers, so everything spilled out the moment you picked them up. And I will be honest with you. I did not have a lot of temperance back then. I was ready to fight. For real. The kind of ready where your body is already moving before your mind has finished deciding. There were other teens watching, a shift to finish, and a job I actually needed. I had to make a call fast. Do I react the way every part of me wants to? I asked myself. Do I let this moment cost me something I can't afford to lose? That was a discernment moment. The stakes were not national. But they were just as real to a teenager counting on that paycheck. And the same principle applied: Pause before you move. Ask what this is actually going to cost you. Don't let someone else's provocation write your next chapter.

Or consider the parent standing at the door watching their child leave for a party at a house they don't know. The hesitation is not about distrust of the child. It is about something they cannot name, a quiet unsettledness, a feeling that something is off. And the world will tell parents they are being overprotective, anxious, controlling. But sometimes that hesitation is not anxiety. Sometimes it is the Spirit speaking in the only register available when there is no time to pray a long prayer. Learning to honor that voice at fourteen, at the front door, or in a government briefing room is the same work. The address changes. The lesson does not.

And then there are the times we do not listen. The moments we override the hesitation, dismiss the unease, say yes because the pressure is too loud or the opportunity looks too good or we simply want to believe we are reading things clearly when we are not. Those moments happen. They happened to David. They happened to Peter. They happened to me.

But here is the truth that has held me together through every misread, every misstep, every yes I should have withheld, and every no I gave too late: God does not discard the people who make the wrong call. He redeems them. The same God who restored Peter after the denial, who used David's later years to produce some of Scripture's most honest poetry, who turned Jonah's detour into the city's salvation, that God is not finished with you because you missed something. Your mistake is not the final word on your discernment. It is data. It is formation. And if you bring it to Him honestly, He has a way of turning even your wrong turns into roads that lead somewhere worth going. Condemnation says You should have known better. Conviction says now you do. One keeps you stuck. The other moves you forward. God is always in the business of the second.

REFLECTION

There are seasons when what we want and what God is asking of us are not aligned. Take a moment to name something you genuinely want right now—an opportunity, a relationship, a role, a season of relief—that you sense God may be asking you to lay down, or at least to hold more loosely. What does your honest response feel like? Not the spiritual answer you would give in a prayer group but the real one. Is there resentment? Grief? Confusion? Bring it. God is not afraid of your honesty, and discernment cannot begin until pretending ends.

Think about a time when you felt something—a quiet unsettledness about a person, a room, an opportunity, an invitation—was off before you could explain it. Did you honor it, or did you override it because you could not prove it? What happened? Whether that moment ended in protection or in a hard lesson, what did it teach you about the cost of trusting—or not trusting—the Spirit's quiet voice? And where in your life right now is that same voice speaking, and you are not yet sure whether to listen?

Finally, think about a decision where you missed it. Not the one you are most ashamed of but one where, in hindsight, you can see clearly that you moved ahead of God or stayed past His release or said yes when the answer in your spirit was already no. What did God do with that? Did He abandon the story, or did He redirect it? Where are you still waiting for Him to redeem something you had broken? Condemnation keeps you rehearsing the mistake. Conviction moves you toward what He is still building. Which one are you living in right now?

PRAYER

Father, teach me to trust Your timing more than my desire. I confess that waiting is hard. That sacrifice is hard. That laying something down I have been holding with both hands is one of the most costly forms of obedience I have ever been asked to practice.

Sharpen my discernment. Teach me to recognize the quiet no of Your Spirit even when I cannot explain it, even when everyone around me is saying yes, even when the opportunity looks legitimate, even when hesitation costs me something I wanted. Protect me from the things I cannot see coming. And give me the humility to honor the unsettledness You place in my spirit before I have the evidence to justify it.

For the times I did not listen—the moments I moved too fast, said yes when You were saying wait or dismissed the quiet warning because I wanted to believe I was reading things clearly—redeem those too. You are not finished with me because I missed something. Condemnation is not Your voice. Conviction is. Speak the second one into every place where I am still rehearsing the first.

In Jesus' mighty name, amen.

My Reflections

Personal notes from Chapter Seven

CHAPTER EIGHT

When Hesitation Is the Sin

So far, we have talked about the costs of saying no throughout this book, but what happens when we become hesitant to provide an answer because we are unsure how God wants us to respond. It is much easier to respond without discernment now and ask for forgiveness later, right? Discernment takes time that busy leaders don't have, right? But discernment is not the end of leadership. It is the beginning of action.

Learning to say no wisely is essential, but it is not sufficient. At some point, leadership requires movement. Decisions must be made. Direction must be given. And clarity must replace hesitation. Indecision—especially when disguised as humility, patience, or caution—can quietly undermine authority, stall progress, and exhaust everyone involved, including the leader.

Scripture is unambiguous on this point. God does not honor perpetual hesitation. He honors leaders who act with courage, clarity, and obedience—even when outcomes are uncertain.

Throughout Scripture, decisive leadership alters the course of history, not because leaders possessed perfect information, but because they trusted God enough to move.

Moses understood this at the Red Sea.

The Israelites were trapped. Pharaoh's army was closing in. Panic spread quickly, as it always does when fear meets uncertainty. Surrender seemed logical and retreat was the emotional response. The sea ahead looked like an immovable barrier. Did Moses call a meeting? No. Did he take a poll? No. He did not delay for further analysis.

He said, "Do not be afraid. Stand firm and you will see the deliverance the Lord will bring you today... The Lord will fight for you; you need only to be still" (Exodus 14:13–14).

He was able to speak so boldly and with authority because he had a relationship with God. He was confident in his actions and his response because of that relationship. How many people today use social media to guide their decisions and rely on likes or comments to determine if something they said or posted was meaningful? I can admit that I have done it. Our confidence in our decisions should come from God and not man.

Moses' decisiveness did not come from confidence in circumstances or the thoughts of the Israelites. It came from confidence in what God had already spoken. Leadership, in that moment, required a clear voice not consensus.

Joshua faced a similar weight when he stepped into leadership after Moses' death. The responsibility was overwhelming. The people were watching. The stakes were high. And God's instruction to him was simple, direct, and repeated for emphasis:

"Be strong and courageous... for the Lord your God will be with you wherever you go" (Joshua 1:9).

Joshua's courage was not emotional bravado. It was obedience in motion. He understood that leadership does not wait for certainty; it moves forward anchored in trust and relationship.

These leaders didn't merely make decisions. They took action that aligned with God's will.

The Cost of Hesitation

Indecision, however, has its own quiet power—and not the kind leaders want.

When hesitation becomes habitual, it carries consequences. Authority weakens, confusion spreads, and trust erodes. People begin filling the vacuum with assumptions, frustrations, and competing agendas. Scripture warns us plainly that "If the trumpet does not sound a clear call, who will get ready for battle?" (1 Corinthians 14:8).

Leadership requires clarity. A leader who avoids decision-making, or who cannot say no decisively, creates instability. Indecision communicates uncertainty, and uncertainty invites disorder.

Decisiveness Is a Discipline

I learned this lesson early in my leadership journey when I stepped into a new organization with a clear mandate: strengthen the team and disrupt patterns that had been normalized for years.

Almost immediately two challenges presented themselves. One employee's behavior clearly warranted disciplinary action. Another had a long-standing issue with tardiness that had gone unaddressed for years. As a new leader, my instinct was to assert authority quickly, to involve human resources, formalize consequences, and establish control. Because that was what should be done in those circumstances, right?

I was new and had to be on my A game. Respect mattered. Credibility mattered. And time mattered.

So I paused. I realized I was standing at a crossroads familiar to many leaders. I could escalate aggressively and risk consuming time and emotional energy better spent elsewhere. I could ignore the issues and allow dysfunction to continue. Or I could choose a path that maintained accountability without derailing the broader mission I had been hired to accomplish.

Instead of leaning on my own instincts, I sought counsel from my supervisor.

She gave simple yet profound advice. It reframed everything. "Pick your battles," she said. "The work you were called to do impacts millions of lives, and you have a short window in which to do it. How much time can you really afford to spend focused on these issues?"

That response was everything I needed to hear in that moment.

Instead of moving immediately toward punitive action, I chose a different approach. I implemented structured counseling, followed by consistent coaching and clear expectations. Accountability was not abandoned, but it was applied with intention rather than impulse.

Over time, the behavior improved, not completely, but trust between us was built. By following my supervisor's advice, I was able to remain focused on the broader vision instead of being consumed by individual disruptions.

That experience taught me something essential: Decisiveness does not always look like force. Sometimes it looks like restraint. Sometimes it looks like redirection. And sometimes it looks like knowing when not to escalate a matter.

Leadership is not about reacting to every problem. It is about stewarding energy wisely.

When Restraint Is the Decision

Jesus modeled this kind of leadership constantly.

He did not respond to every accusation. He did not engage every critic. He did not heal every person who demanded it. Scripture tells us that Jesus understood timing and mission so clearly that He often withdrew when others expected Him to advance. Jesus understood that His hour had not yet come. (John 7:6).

That was not avoidance. It was authority.

Decisiveness is not a personality trait reserved for the bold or outspoken. It is a practiced discipline. Being clear in your yeses and your nos will help alleviate drama and build trust in you as a leader, whether you are leading an organization or your family. Discipline, like a muscle, grows and strengthens when leaders clarify their values, anchor decisions in prayer, seek wise counsel, and refuse to be ruled by urgency. "Plans fail for lack of counsel, but with many advisers they succeed" (Proverbs 15:22).

God does not call leaders to be impulsive. But He does call them to be clear.

Discernment without action becomes stagnation. Wisdom without movement becomes frustration. Leadership requires the courage to decide—sometimes imperfectly, often prayerfully, but always obediently.

There is another kind of struggle worth naming here—one that does not get talked about as often as people-pleasing but is just as common and just as costly.

Consider a woman I'll call Angela. Angela was talented. Her gifts were visible to her mentors, to her supervisors, to the people who had watched her work for years and quietly wondered when she would step into the role she was clearly made for. Doors opened for Angela with a kind of regularity that might have looked like blessings from the outside.

But Angela had a pattern. Every time a door opened, every time an opportunity arrived that would require her to step into something larger, something more visible, something that would ask her to trust herself in a new arena, she found a reason to wait. The timing wasn't right. She needed more preparation. She didn't want to seem presumptuous. What if she wasn't actually ready? What if she stepped through and found out, on the other side, that the gift everyone else saw in her was something she couldn't actually deliver?

Angela never said no dramatically. She simply delayed. She asked for more time. She deferred to someone else who seemed more qualified, more polished, more certain. And in the meantime, the doors she hesitated in front of opened for other people—not because God had closed them, but because Angela had stood in them long enough that someone else walked through.

Angela's struggle was not with people-pleasing. It was with herself. With the voice that told her she was not enough for what God was offering. With the fear that saying yes to an open door would expose something she had worked very hard to keep hidden—the quiet certainty that she was one step away from being found out as less than everyone believed her to be.

This chapter has been about learning to say no to opportunities that are not yours. But Angela's story is the other side of the same lesson: Saying no to what God is genuinely offering is also a failure of discernment. Not every hesitation is wisdom. Sometimes it is fear wearing the clothes of humility.

Maybe you are not new to your field, your ministry, or your community. Maybe you have been standing in front of open doors for years. Maybe someone believed in you more than you believed in yourself, and you found a reason to step back. Ask yourself honestly: Is there an opportunity you have been sitting on, calling it patience, calling it preparation, calling it waiting on God when the truth is that God already opened the door and fear has kept you from walking through? God does not open doors to embarrass you. He opens them because He has already equipped you for what is on the other side.

REFLECTION

Leadership without discernment eventually collapses under its own pace. Before you move on, sit with this question: What decision have you been delaying, and what is the true cost of that delay not just to you but to the people and the vision waiting on the other side of your answer? Sometimes what we call wisdom is actually avoidance wearing a more respectable name. Is there a decision God has already made clear that you have been slow to execute because of fear of judgment, fear of conflict, or fear of being wrong? What has that slowness protected, and what has it cost?

And now the harder question: Are you more like Angela than you have been willing to admit? Is there a door—an opportunity, a calling, a role, an invitation—that God has opened that you have been standing in front of? What is the one step—not the whole journey, just the next step—that you could take this week toward the thing God has already equipped you for? What would you need to believe about yourself, and about Him, to take it?

PRAYER

Lord, grant me the clarity and courage to lead with wisdom. Not the kind of wisdom that waits for perfect information before taking a step but the kind that holds a decision in prayer long enough to know whether it is Yours before moving forward with it.

Help me make decisions that honor Your will before they honor my reputation. Teach me to lead from abundance, from a place of clarity and trust rather than from scarcity, fear, or the need to appear unshakeable. Where I have been indecisive out of fear, give me courage. Where I have been decisive out of pride, give me humility.

And show me where You have already opened a door and I have been standing in front of it calling my hesitation patience. Remind me that You do not prepare people and then abandon them at the threshold. Let my leadership reflect Your order, Your peace, and Your purpose not my urgency, my image, or my need to be seen as ready.

In Jesus' mighty name, amen.

My Reflections

Personal notes from Chapter Eight

CHAPTER NINE

Yes, No, and the Wounds That Shape Our Choices

Most of us don't struggle with saying no because we lack wisdom. If wisdom were the issue, many of us would have solved this long ago. The real struggle runs deeper than intellect or discipline.

We struggle because we fear rejection—and because we fear what rejection might say about us.

So we say yes at the PTA meeting even though our calendar is already hanging on by a thread. We say yes at work because we don't want to be that employee—the one who quietly stops getting invited into the room. We say yes in relationships because no feels risky, and the possibility of being misunderstood, disliked, or worst of all unwanted feels heavier than the cost of overextending ourselves.

And if we're honest, many of those yeses aren't rooted in generosity at all.

They're rooted in fear.

Fear Wearing the Face of Kindness

Fear has a way of disguising itself as kindness. It sounds polite. It looks cooperative. It even feels responsible—for a moment. Fear-based yeses, however, rarely end in peace. More often, they end in resentment, exhaustion, and that quiet, familiar ache that whispers, oops I did it again. I abandoned myself again.

There is a very specific kind of shame that follows a yes you never should have given. It doesn't announce itself loudly. It doesn't accuse with force. It whispers.

You feel it in your spirit before you can name it. Something feels off. Then it creeps into your thoughts. Why did I do that again? Eventually, it settles into your heart and asks the question we dread most: What does this say about me?

That is usually the moment the enemy leans in.

The Shame That Follows

Scripture tells us plainly that "the thief comes only to steal and kill and destroy" (John 10:10). And often, he doesn't steal our faith all at once. He steals our confidence, our voice, and our sense of belonging—one shame-filled moment at a time.

Shame doesn't just make us feel bad. It makes us quiet. It convinces us that distance from God is safer than honesty with Him. And once shame takes hold, the cycle tightens its grip. Fear leads to yes. Yes leads to shame. Shame leads to silence.

And silence is exactly where the enemy wants us.

When I said yes once out of fear instead of obedience—when I agreed simply to avoid discomfort, rejection, or conflict—it didn't bring peace afterward. It brought a quiet, internal unease. A sense that I compromised something I didn't need to. And that sense of disobedience didn't draw me closer to God.

It made me feel unworthy of Him. Church felt uncomfortable. Conviction felt heavy instead of loving. Prayer felt awkward—like I didn't quite belong in the conversation anymore.

So I pulled back. It wasn't rebellion. It was shame — and shame is a liar that sounds a lot like wisdom. That is the subtle danger of fear-based yeses. They rarely push us away from God loudly. They do it quietly, through shame.

Shame always follows a familiar script. You should know better. You've gone too far.

And the enemy tells you that God must be disappointed in you now. We all know that story.

God Does Not Withdraw

Scripture tells a very different story. It tells us that "there is now no condemnation for those who are in Christ Jesus" (Romans 8:1).

While condemnation pushes us away from God, conviction draws us back to Him. And if what you feel after a misaligned yes is a pull to hide, withdraw, or stay silent, that is not God speaking. That is the enemy trying to keep you disconnected from truth, authority, and healing.

The Bible is full of people who said yes when they should have said no. Peter denied Jesus—not once but three times—because he was afraid of rejection. David acted out of impulse and desire. Some of us, like the reluctant prophet, have run hard in the opposite direction—not from confusion but from the weight of knowing exactly what God is asking.

And yet God abandoned none of them.

What changed their trajectory wasn't perfection. It wasn't self-punishment or spiritual theatrics. It was repentance, turning back toward truth. "The Lord is close to the brokenhearted and saves those who are crushed in spirit" (Psalm 34:18).

God does not withdraw when we fail. He moves closer.

The way out of the shame spiral isn't trying harder to get it right next time. It's truth. Truth that says your identity is not defined by your worst yes. Truth that says God's love is not revoked by your misalignment. Truth that reminds you that you are still allowed to choose differently.

Repentance isn't about beating yourself up. It's about turning around. And every time we turn back toward God, we reclaim a little more voice, a little more authority, and a little more peace.

You Are Not Saying No to Earn Love

Learning to say no without apologizing for existing takes practice. It isn't about harshness or rigidity. It's about clarity.

Sometimes clarity sounds like, "Let me pray about that." Sometimes it sounds like, "That doesn't work for me." And sometimes it sounds like silence because you don't owe everyone an explanation.

There are moments when saying no feels uncomfortable because it exposes a fear you didn't realize was driving you. When that happens, pause. Ask yourself what you are truly afraid will happen if you don't say yes. Then bring that fear to God before it makes the decision for you. Remember, "If God is for us, who can be against us?" (Romans 8:31).

You are already accepted. Already loved. Already chosen.

You are not saying no to earn love. You are saying no because you are loved.

Ecclesiastes tells us there is a time for everything—a time to keep and a time to let go. Saying yes out of fear is still fear, even when it looks polite, responsible, or kind. But saying no in obedience, that is worship because every no aligned with God's truth makes room for peace, freedom, and the right yes to follow.

Take a moment and consider where you've said yes out of fear of rejection. Notice what shame followed and what lie you believed afterward. Then ask yourself what boundary God has been gently prompting you to set—not in anger but in love.

Consider a young woman I'll call Maya. Fresh out of college, degree in hand, Maya had every reason to step boldly into her next chapter. She was intelligent, capable, and deeply loved by the people around her. Beneath the confidence she projected a pattern she had inherited long before she ever set foot on a campus.

Maya grew up in a home where love was conditional. Approval came when she was agreeable, quiet, and useful and quietly disappeared when she pushed back or told the truth about what she needed. By the time she graduated, she had no memory of ever being taught that her no mattered. She just knew, in the way the body knows things before the mind names them, that disagreeing cost her something she could not afford to lose.

Her struggle didn't show up at work. Maya was surprisingly capable of holding professional lines. It was in her closest relationships—with her mother, with friends, with the man she was beginning to love—where the pattern lived. The people who mattered most were the people she could least afford to disappoint. So she kept saying yes. Yes to conversations that reopened old wounds. Yes to being the one who managed the family's emotional temperature. Yes to showing up for everyone else before she had finished showing up for herself.

What Maya eventually understood—slowly, through prayer and honest reflection—was that her yes in those relationships wasn't generosity. It was self-protection. As long as she kept giving, she couldn't be accused of withholding. As long as she kept showing up, no one could leave. Her yes was a wall built from old fear not an offering built from love.

Healing for Maya didn't begin with learning to say no. It began with learning to ask where the yes was coming from. When she could trace the fear underneath the compliance, she could bring it to God—not as a flaw to be ashamed of but as a wound to be tended. And slowly, she began to discover that her no, offered with love and grounded in prayer, did not destroy the relationships she had spent years trying to protect. In most cases, it deepened them.

Maybe you are not fresh out of college. Maybe your version of this story is set in a boardroom, a marriage, a ministry, or a friendship that has stretched for decades. Ask yourself honestly: Are there relationships in your life where your yes is not really an offering but is actually a wall? Where the fear underneath is not "what will happen to them" but "what will happen to me" if I stop giving? That is not faithfulness. That is fear that has learned to dress well. And God is not asking you to maintain it. He is asking you to bring it to Him.

REFLECTION

Fear of rejection is one of the oldest weights we carry, and one of the most powerful forces shaping our decisions. Before you move forward, sit with this: In what specific relationship, role, or environment do you notice yourself most consistently saying yes when your spirit is saying something different? Name it as precisely as you can, not in a vague sense of being a people-pleaser but the actual situation, the actual person, the actual dynamic where your desire for belonging consistently outweighs your capacity to be honest. What is it about that specific space that makes your no feel most dangerous?

Consider Maya's question for yourself. In the relationships that matter most to you, is your yes really an offering or is it a wall? Are you giving because love moves you to or because fear of what happens when you stop is what actually drives you? Think about a wound from your past that may still be shaping your response to potential rejection today. An early experience of being left out, dismissed, or unwanted. What do you do now to make sure it doesn't happen again? Is that response still serving you, or is it now the very thing standing between you and the freedom God is offering? What would it look like to bring that specific wound to God this week—not to be fixed immediately but to be held honestly?

Father, forgive me for the times I said yes out of fear instead of obedience. Forgive me for the habitual, deeply worn grooves of agreement that I have mistaken for generosity, for kindness, for the way a good person shows up. Heal the shame that followed those yeses.

Restore my confidence in Your love, a love that does not change based on what I produce. Help me receive it so completely that I no longer need the approval of others to feel like I am enough. Where rejection has taught me to shrink, speak the truth about my worth in language I can actually hear.

Give me the courage to honor the convictions You place within me—even when honoring them costs me someone's good opinion, someone's presence, or someone's comfort with who I am becoming. Remind me in those moments that You are not asking me to earn belonging. You are asking me to trust that I already have it . . . in You.

In Jesus' mighty name, amen.

My Reflections

CHAPTER TEN

The Weight of Every Title

Someone gave you a list of titles before you were old enough to decide whether you wanted them or not:

Daughter.

Sister.

Friend.

Wife.

Mother.

Caregiver.

Backbone.

Stronghold.

The one who holds it together.

The one who never falls apart.

The one people call when everything is on fire.

The one who answers.

That list is not just long. It is sacred. It is inherited. It comes from grandmothers who worked through grief and kept cooking. Mothers who never asked for help and never admitted they needed it. Communities that praised endurance and equated vulnerability with failure. Churches that celebrated self-sacrifice while quietly judging anyone who couldn't keep up the pace.

And somewhere in the middle of all of that, you were handed someone else's gift and told it was your responsibility.

Titles and the Wounds They Carry

In earlier chapters we have explored the wounds that drive our yeses—the fear of rejection, the trauma that taught us our no didn't matter, the shame that follows a misaligned decision. Those are real, and they matter. Let's talk about something quieter and in some ways more insidious: the titles we carry not because of fear or trauma but because of love. The expectations we absorbed not through wounds but through inheritance. The gifts we performed not because something forced us to but because we never stopped to question whether they were ours to carry at all.

So what happens when we say yes to who people expect us to be and no to who God actually made us to be?

The Weight I Didn't Talk About

I have to tell you something I did not talk about anywhere else in this book. When I had my first set of twins, I was not ready for what came next. I was married. I was capable. I loved my children fiercely. And I fell apart anyway.

Postpartum depression does not care about your credentials, your intentions, or your love. It does not ask whether you are Black or white, educated or not, married or not. It comes in quiet and takes things you didn't know you could lose—including the instinct to reach for your own babies.

I pulled away. I became distant. There were days when I did not want to touch them and then immediately there was shame. Because what kind of mother doesn't want to hold her children? What kind of woman, who wanted these children, who prayed for them, who had a husband and a home—what kind of woman falls apart like this?

For me, that shame wore a specific face. I was young and Black, and I already knew what the world assumed about young Black mothers. I had fought against those assumptions my entire life. I had done everything right. And still something was wrong, and I was not going to let anyone see it. This silence was not the silence of someone too busy to slow down. It was the silence of a woman whose pride was standing between her and her babies. Asking for help felt like confirmation of everything I had spent years refusing to become in other people's eyes.

So I said no to help. I said no to honesty. I said no to the support that might have shortened the distance between me and my babies, all because my pride was louder than my pain.

That silence cost me. It cost my children. It cost us years of connection that we are still rebuilding, carefully and lovingly, to this day.

And then, twenty-two months later, I was mobilized for Operation Iraqi Freedom.

I want you to sit with that for a moment. Twenty-two months. My babies were barely out of infancy when I deployed. The disconnect that had already begun in those hard early months became a chasm, and filling it required more grace, more time, and more intentional love than I could have imagined.

I am not telling you this for sympathy. I am telling you this because I know I am not the only one.

There are women reading this right now who gave everything they had to everyone in their lives and said no to themselves so consistently and so silently that they eventually had nothing left. Women who performed so capably and convincingly that no one knew they were drowning. Women who confused responsibility with giftedness and spent years trying to be what they were never made to be—and shaming themselves for failing at it.

I have been that woman.

Years later, a pastor's wife said something to me that I have carried with me ever since. She said: "We all have gifts and we all have responsibilities. Being a mother is your responsibility. But nurturing everyone, that is a gift. And not every mother has that gift."

I needed her to say that twice before it landed.

Because what I had been doing—what so many of us do—was saying yes to someone else's gift while ignoring my own. I had seen women who moved through rooms touching people, pulling children close, mothering every lost soul they encountered, and I had spent years measuring my love against theirs and finding myself lacking. I thought that being a good mother meant being a super nurturer. I thought love looked like that specific expression of itself.

What I had not understood is that love takes many forms, and God distributes the gifts accordingly.

Romans 12:6 tells us plainly that "we have different gifts, according to the grace given to each of us." That verse applies to ministry. It applies to leadership. And yes, it applies to how we love.

You can be a fiercely devoted mother without being gifted as a nurturer of everyone. You can love your children deeply without it looking like someone else's love. You can show up faithfully in your responsibility without pretending to carry a gift God gave to someone else.

The problem is not that you are missing something. The problem is that you have been trying to operate in a gift that was never yours, and calling yourself a failure for not thriving in it.

The Myth of the Strong Black Woman

For Black women especially, the pressure to be strong is real.

The strong Black woman is not just a cultural archetype—she is a generational assignment, passed down with love but also with a cost. She does not break. She does not need. She holds the family, the church, the community, the workplace together with whatever she has left. She does not complain. We were not only handed someone else's gift. We were handed someone else's definition of strength.

That mythology has saved lives. It has built families and carried legacies across impossible terrain.

It has also silenced suffering. It has delayed healing. It has taught whole generations of women that asking for help is weakness, that vulnerability is betrayal, and that their value is in their endurance.

But Scripture never tells us that. Not once.

What Scripture tells us is that we are one body with many parts, and that no part can say to another, "I don't need you." It tells us that we are to carry each other's burdens, which means we are allowed to have them. It tells us that when we are weak, God is strong, which means we are permitted to be weak.

Saying no to the myth of the woman who never needs anything is not weakness. It is obedience to the God who designed you to need community, to carry specific gifts, and to ask for help when the weight exceeds what He gave you to carry alone.

You do not have to be everything to everyone. You were not designed to be. The version of you that tries to be everything is the version that slowly disappears—from herself, from her children, from the God who made her for something more specific and more beautiful than exhaustion.

Your responsibility is real. Your calling is yours. But the gift belongs to God, and He decides who carries it.

What God Actually Put in You

Say no to the title that was never yours.

Say no to the pressure to use a gift God gave to someone else.

Say no to the shame that told you something was wrong with you for not thriving in it.

Then ask God—quietly, honestly—what He actually put in you. Because it is there. It has always been there. And it is more than enough.

REFLECTION

Before you move forward, take a moment with the following question and answer it honestly, not with the version of yourself you present to the world but the one only you and God can see: What title are you carrying that was handed to you by others rather than given to you by God? What role did you absorb from your family, your culture, your church, your community because it was expected and because saying no to it felt like betrayal? ". Name it. And then ask honestly: Is the weight of that title costing you the presence God intended you to have in the roles you were called to?

Now think about the specific expression of love or strength that you have been measuring yourself against and finding yourself lacking. Whose gift have you been trying to perform? What would it look like to lay down that comparison today—not as resignation but as relief? And finally: if a woman you loved came to you carrying the same shame you have been carrying, the same quiet certainty that something was wrong with her because she could not thrive in a gift God never gave her, what would you say to her? Say that to yourself now. You need to hear it just as much as she would.

PRAYER

Lord, I come to You carrying titles I did not choose and expectations I did not create. I come carrying the weight of who I was supposed to be—the woman who holds everything, who needs nothing, who endures without asking for relief and serves without requiring acknowledgment.

Forgive me for the times I said no to requests for help due to my pride, when the cost of that refusal fell on the people I love most. Forgive me for the silence that looked like strength but was really just isolation and the refusal to let anyone see what I was actually carrying because I had learned to believe that being seen meant being weak.

Teach me the difference between my responsibility and my gift. Help me show up faithfully for what is mine to carry and lay down without shame what was never mine to begin with. For every woman reading this who has been holding too much for too long remind her, as You remind me, that You were never supposed to be carried. You came to carry us.

In Jesus' mighty name, amen.

My Reflections

Personal notes from Chapter Ten

CHAPTER ELEVEN

When Yes Feeds Obedience—or Excess

Yes is not a one-dimensional word.

It can be casual or consequential, hesitant or wholehearted. Sometimes it slips out reflexively—"sure," "okay," "I guess so"—without much thought attached. Other times, it is spoken with full awareness that life will never look the same afterward. Every yes carries weight, but not every yes carries the same intention, and not every yes feeds the same thing.

Because of that, understanding the spectrum of yes forces us to slow down and ask a deeper question, one we rarely pause long enough to consider.

What am I feeding when I say yes?

Every yes nourishes something. The real question is whether it is nourishing obedience or excess.

For much of my life, yes came easily. Again as a mother of six, availability was not just expected; it was required. Add to that the many other hats I wore, and dependability became part of my identity. Saying yes felt responsible. It felt productive. It felt loving.

It also felt fast.

I don't like to be late, nor do I like to keep people waiting. I value efficiency, decisiveness, and follow-through to the point of feeling obsessive about it and I have been rewarded for those traits. But what I had to learn, often through exhaustion and frustration, is that not procrastinating is not the same as godly reflection. Both can exist, but they are not interchangeable.

Looking back, I can see how easily I used efficiency as an excuse to rush answers that deserved prayer. I confused speed with wisdom. And while my intentions were good, some of my yeses were spoken before discernment had time to speak.

Scripture reminds us—gently but firmly—that we are to be "quick to listen, slow to speak" (James 1:19). That instruction is not about hesitation for hesitation's sake; it is about restraint in a world that rewards immediacy. Careful reflection done in God's time saves us from commitments that quietly drain our peace and distort our priorities.

There is also a sin Scripture names that we rarely examine because it feels too ordinary and too socially acceptable: gluttony.

Most of us were taught to think of gluttony as overeating. But biblically, it is far broader. It is excess without restraint. It is saying yes to more—more comfort, more productivity, more affirmation, more distraction—without asking whether that more is coming from God.

This is where gluttony and misplaced yeses intersect. Every unexamined yes feeds something, and every undiscerned yes consumes something.

Scripture explains the danger clearly when it says, "Like a city whose walls are broken through is a person who lacks self-control" (Proverbs 25:28). In biblical times, walls meant protection. A city without them was exposed and vulnerable. In the same way, a life without restraint leaves the heart unguarded.

Paul echoes this when he writes that some people's "god is their stomach... and their mind is set on earthly things" (Philippians 3:19). This is not condemnation of desire; it is a warning about desire ruling identity. Anything we cannot say no to has the power to become a functional god. Scripture names this plainly when it warns against "greed, which is idolatry" (Colossians 3:5).

One of the ways I try to guard against this kind of excess—especially when decisions come quickly—is by filtering my agreements through Scripture before they ever reach my mouth. Philippians 4:8 became more than a verse to me; it became a practice.

Because I love a good acronym, I use what I call LEARNT PP, which comes from Philippians 4:8. I ask myself whether what I am about to agree to is

Lovely Does this bring beauty, harmony, or goodness, or does it quietly cost you your peace? Example: If saying yes leaves you resentful, exhausted, and short-tempered with the people you love most, it is not lovely. Lovely doesn't require perfection, but it should leave something better than it found it.

Excellent. Is this the best use of what God has entrusted to you—your time, your gifts, your energy? Example: Excellence isn't doing everything well. It's doing the right things well. If saying yes to this means doing something else—your children, your health, your calling— poorly, it may not be excellent in God's economy.

Admirable. Would you be at peace if God, and those whose wisdom you respect, could see exactly why you said yes? Example: If the real reason you're saying yes is to be seen, to avoid conflict, or to earn approval you should already know you have, that motive may not pass the admirable test.

Good Report. Does this hold up to the light for your faith, your family, and your witness? Example: If this yes became a headline, would it honor God? Of good report means it doesn't just look right from the outside; it is right from the inside out.

Noble. Is this worthy of who God says you are and what He has called you to? Example: Some requests, though not sinful, are simply beneath your calling. Noble asks whether this yes is consistent with your character and your dignity—not just whether it's permissible.

True. Are you being honest with yourself about why you're really saying yes? Example: Are you saying yes because it's aligned with your purpose or because you're afraid of what happens if you say no? Truth asks you to examine your own motives before you open your mouth.

Praiseworthy. Would God be glorified by this yes? Does it point beyond you to something greater? Example: If the outcome of your yes leads people toward God through your service, your integrity, or your faithfulness, it may be praiseworthy. If it draws attention only to you or feeds something that doesn't honor Him, pause.

Pure. Are your intentions clean, free from hidden agendas, mixed motives, or quiet compromise? Example: Pure doesn't mean perfect. It means uncomplicated by self-interest. Ask yourself: if no one ever found out I said yes to this, would I still do it? If the answer is no, that's a purity check worth taking seriously.

If a yes does not pass that filter, it usually is not meant to pass my lips.

Discernment is not only about what we decide. It is also about what we allow to occupy our minds. I return to some of these Scriptures intentionally and often because repetition in Scripture is not redundant. It is emphasis. God repeats what we are prone to forget, so I do too.

Esau is one of those reminders.

Hungry, exhausted, and impatient, Esau said yes to a bowl of stew and no to his birthright. Scripture tells us he despised it—not because it lacked value, but because hunger screamed louder than legacy. His yes was not immoral. It was impulsive. And it cost him something he could never recover.

Can you imagine giving up your divine calling, your dream career, your children, and family for something as fleeting as a bowl of soup? We don't know what we are giving up when we say yes to one more thing that God did not approve, but one thing I can say is that we can never get that time back. Time missed with our loved ones. Time we missed in taking care of our health. This is not meant to condemn you or Esau. Listen, Esau did not fail because he was evil. He failed because he would not endure discomfort long enough to protect what was sacred.

I wish I could say this kind of failure shows up only in moments of obvious temptation. But sometimes it appears in seasons of obedience that simply do not feel fulfilling.

There is a kind of yes Scripture does not glamorize—a yes that is not bold, visible, or immediately rewarding. It is the yes of restraint. The yes of staying. The yes of obedience without fulfillment.

I learned this in a season when my life looked steady on the outside but felt small on the inside. I had spent years advocating for people, for policy, and for systems that needed reform. Then God placed me in a role where my voice was intentionally restrained. The work required neutrality, precision, patience, and silence. I was called to it, but I did not feel fulfilled by it.

At first, I assumed something was wrong. I told myself my gifts were being wasted. But over time, I began to recognize what God was doing. He was strengthening my attention to detail. He was teaching me how to sit in discomfort without rushing toward relief. He was forming discernment that did not depend on affirmation or visibility.

Then an opportunity came that looked great on paper—leadership, influence, familiar ground. I prayed, expecting peace. Instead, there was only noise. So I said no.

That no surprised me. I knew I could do the work, but for some reason, I was not supposed to.

The thing to remember is that not every good opportunity is holy ground. And not every yes that feels powerful is obedient.

That season taught me something I had never fully understood before: Sometimes discernment does not ask us to choose between right and wrong. Sometimes it asks us to choose between movement and formation, between personal fulfillment and calling.

Moses understood this long before he stood before Pharaoh. He spent decades in the wilderness because restraint was part of his preparation. Before God trusted him with deliverance, He trusted him with obscurity. And what may have felt like punishment was in fact preparation.

> *Temptation rarely asks for everything at once. It asks for access.*

Still, not every yes is neutral. Some yeses quietly place us in agreement with temptation.

Take Samson. Samson's downfall did not begin with Delilah. It began with small, repeated yeses—yes to proximity, yes to indulgence, yes to testing boundaries he had already been warned not to cross. Each yes weakened his discernment. When his strength left him, it was not taken suddenly; it had been surrendered incrementally.

Temptation rarely asks for everything at once. It asks for access.

James teaches that desire conceives, action follows, and consequences are then born. The danger is not desire itself. It is agreement without restraint. When we say yes to what God has already cautioned us about, we are no longer discerning; we are rationalizing.

But Scripture offers hope. God promises that no temptation comes without a way out. There is always a ram in the bush. That is why we are told to flee—not analyze, test, or negotiate with temptation. Discernment is not about proving how strong we are. It is about protecting what God is growing within us and for us.

And it doesn't stop there. There is also something that happens to discernment when we are wounded.

Take our physical bodies for example. Have you ever stubbed your toe on the corner of the wall—ouch—and suddenly it's red and starting to swell? It turns red and swells because blood is rushing to that injured spot to help heal it.

And what sometimes happens in that moment—when your brain realizes something painful just happened to your foot—you stop running on reason and start running on instinct. You might even shout an expletive or two.

When the body experiences injury, survival becomes the priority. And when survival becomes the priority, whatever is in you tends to come out—because there is no longer enough rational space to restrain it.

Spiritually, the same thing happens.

When we are wounded by loss, betrayal, fear, or trauma, discernment pulls back and instinct takes over. We grasp for relief. We decide quickly. We say yes not because it is wise, but because pain demands resolution.

I learned this the hard way. After a season of deep personal trauma, my discernment became fragile in ways I did not immediately recognize. My sense of safety had been disrupted, and I found myself making agreements not from clarity but from the quiet desire to feel grounded again.

In that season, some of my yeses were not rooted in wisdom. They were rooted in survival. And while they gave me a temporary sense of control, they did not bring the healing I needed. I was not operating from discernment. I was operating from injury. And injury always prioritizes relief over alignment.

Peter understood this tension. In the garden, he said yes to violence and no to restraint. Hours later, under fear and pressure, he said no three times to the very Savior he loved. His responses were not rooted in discernment. They were driven by fear.

But Peter was restored because his failure to discern did not disqualify his calling just like it doesn't disqualify our callings.

One of the most meaningful yeses of my life was law school—but only after surrender.

For years, every time I said I wanted to go, I ended up pregnant. Eventually, I stopped saying it altogether. I was not ready for another set of twins! I finally prayed honestly and asked God for one thing. "If this is Your will," I prayed, "I do not want to go into debt." God answered swiftly and with clarity. I was accepted shortly after applying, and I graduated debt-free.

So you see, a faithful yes is marked not by ease but by fruit. And it is not marked by speed but by peace.

Scripture tells us to "let the peace of Christ rule in your hearts" (Colossians 3:15). Peace does not mean the road will be smooth, but it does mean you are on the right one.

Jesus speaks plainly when He says, "Let your 'Yes' be yes, and your 'No,' no" (Matthew 5:37 NKJV). James repeats the same instruction: "All you need to say is a simple "Yes" or "No" (James 5:12). Together, they remind us that integrity does not require explanation, and obedience does not need persuasion.

Clarity can stand on its own.

*So the question becomes not Can I say
yes? but Should I?*

What am I feeding with this agreement: obedience or excess? Calling or appetite?

A wise yes nourishes obedience. An unexamined yes feeds excess. And discernment is the difference.

REFLECTION

In this chapter, we were asked to examine the difference between a yes that feeds obedience and a yes that feeds excess. Before you move forward, take an honest look at the yeses you are currently carrying—not the ones you agreed to in faith and have seen produce fruit but the ones that quietly drain. Look at the commitments that have outlasted the clarity that created them and the obligations that were once right and may no longer be. Which of your current yeses are nourishing your calling and which are simply feeding your appetite for approval, productivity, or belonging, or the relief of not having to deal with a difficult conversation?

Now consider the role of hunger in your decision-making. Where in your life have you been consuming—affirmation, opportunity, engagement, activity—without ever stopping to ask whether you are satisfied or simply full? There is a difference. Satisfaction is the fruit of alignment. Fullness is sometimes just the result of excess. And consider what God may be protecting in you through the invitation to slow down or restrain. What is being formed in you in the space between desire and fulfillment that would not be formed if you simply received everything you wanted, immediately? Restraint, when practiced faithfully, is not deprivation. It is formation. What formation might God be doing in you right now that requires a slower pace than you would choose for yourself?

Lord, teach me to discern my yeses as carefully as my nos. When urgency feels loud and restraint feels costly, quiet my spirit enough to hear You clearly. I have not always paused before agreeing. I have not always asked whether what I was feeding was obedience—or simply appetite dressed in spiritual language.

Forgive me for the excess I have dressed in the language of service. For the times I kept going not because You called me to keep going but because stopping required a kind of honesty I was not ready to offer. Protect me in seasons of vulnerability, when pain tries to decide for me and relief masquerades as wisdom.

Let my yeses honor You. Let my nos protect what You have entrusted to me. And let the space between the two be filled not with anxiety or second-guessing but with the steady confidence of someone who knows the difference between a calling and a craving—and trusts You enough to honor that difference.

In Jesus' mighty name, amen.

My Reflections

Personal notes from Chapter Eleven

CHAPTER TWELVE

When Escape Looks Like Yes

There have been seasons when I wanted to say yes to escape. Yes to distance. Yes to walking away from what felt heavy, disappointing, or deeply uncomfortable. There were moments in my decades of marriage when happiness felt nonexistent, when connection felt strained, when the work required to stay felt far greater than the work required to leave.

And the world makes leaving look easy, doesn't it?

Divorce is no longer whispered about—it's normalized. Reinvention is celebrated. Starting over is framed as brave, whereas staying during trying times is viewed as weak. When feelings shift, culture tells us that commitment is optional. We're told that if something no longer brings us happiness, it must no longer be right. That discomfort is a sign to exit, and endurance is outdated.

In fact, we've gone so far in this direction that people now throw divorce parties complete with balloons, cakes, and congratulations. The ending of a covenant is treated like a graduation. Loss is reframed as liberation. What was once mourned is now marketed as empowerment.

If you are already tired, already lonely, already hurting, that messaging is powerful and enticing. It whispers that relief is just one decision away. That peace can be achieved by cutting ties. That happiness is found on the other side of walking away. In moments like that, saying yes to escape feels not only tempting, it feels reasonable. Even justified.

I want to be clear and careful here, because this matters.

As an attorney, I have walked with people through divorce, and I know firsthand that even when there is laughter, relief, or celebration on the outside, divorce is still a sobering and often deeply painful experience. Ending a marriage is rarely as simple as it looks from the surface. Even when separation is necessary, it usually carries grief, loss, and the weight of what didn't turn out the way anyone hoped.

So hear me clearly. There is no shame in marking a new chapter of your life. There is no condemnation in acknowledging survival, relief, or even joy after a season of pain. This message is mainly for those who find themselves at the crossroads right now still deciding, still weary, still wondering whether staying or leaving is the faithful next step. It's for those who are still in the middle—tired, worn down, discouraged—who feel like they are done fighting, not because the situation is unsafe, but because staying feels harder than leaving. It's for those who are tempted to say yes to separation simply because it seems easier than sitting with unhappiness, discomfort, or the slow work of transformation.

And it is for those moments when exhaustion whispers that escape is wisdom, when relief masquerades as healing, and when walking away feels like the only way to breathe again.

If that is you, this is not a word of judgment. It is an invitation to pause, to discern, to ask whether God is calling you to leave, or whether He is asking you to stay present long enough for something deeper to form.

Ease is not the same as obedience. And relief is not the same as healing.

Sometimes the hardest no we are called to say is not to another person but to a version of ourselves that wants the pain to end immediately, regardless of the long-term cost.

If I'm honest, there were days when that message felt tempting to me. When obedience felt slow and escape felt efficient. When staying looked like stagnation, and leaving looked like growth. But Scripture rarely aligns with what feels easy.

I've learned that there is a difference between saying no to opportunity because of fear and saying no because of faith. There is also a difference between endurance and endurance without discernment. God never asks us to stay where there is abuse, danger, or ongoing unrepentant betrayal. Scripture makes room for protection, separation, and safety. Jesus Himself acknowledged sexual immorality, where a marriage covenant has already been violated, as grounds for divorce. Scripture never commands anyone to remain in harm.

But that truth exists alongside another one we don't talk about enough: Not every desire to leave comes from a place of discernment. Sometimes it's discomfort. Sometimes it's fatigue. Sometimes it's wounded pride. Sometimes it's the exhaustion that comes from living in a fallen world and expecting relationships to always feel fulfilling.

I had to confront that reality in myself.

There were times I wanted to walk away, not because my marriage was unsafe but because it was inconvenient. Because it required humility. Because it demanded patience. Because it exposed areas of selfishness I would rather not face. And I wasn't happy or feeling fulfilled.

That's when obedience became personal.

God never promised any of us constant happiness. He promised presence. And He promised us the fruits of the Spirit, one of which is joy. And I had to learn the difference.

Happiness often asks, "How do I feel right now?"

Joy asks, "Where is God in this, and who is He forming me to be?"

Happiness says, "Leave when it hurts."

Joy says, "Stay present long enough to see what God is doing."

Happiness chases relief.

Joy sustains faith.

This isn't a call to endure what is unsafe or destructive. It is an invitation to discern whether saying yes to walking out the door is rooted in wisdom or simply in discomfort that God may be using to shape us.

Scripture never tells us that obedience will always feel good. It tells us that obedience will be fruitful. Joy, unlike happiness, is not tied to comfort; it's tied to trust. It's why Paul could describe himself as sorrowful yet always rejoicing. It's why Jesus endured the cross for the joy set before Him—not because the cross felt good, but because obedience mattered more than relief.

I had to wrestle with that truth not just in marriage but in family relationships too. There were moments I wanted to cut people off because alignment felt exhausting. Because praying for change felt slower than withdrawing. Because distance felt cleaner than discernment.

But God kept pressing the same question into my spirit: Are you guarding your heart or avoiding transformation?

It is easier to say no to people than to say no to pride. Easier to sever than to intercede. Easier to withdraw than to wait.

When Resistance Is Part of the Plan

Like David refusing to take the throne before God released it, sometimes the most faithful thing we can do is refuse the exit door—even when it's standing wide open.

But perhaps no story captures this more powerfully than the one Israel lived through on the other side of the Red Sea.

Pharaoh hardened his heart repeatedly, resisting God's instruction again and again. Scripture tells us that later God allowed that hardness to continue not to destroy Israel but to reveal His power. Had Pharaoh softened immediately, the Israelites would have left quietly. There would have been no pursuit. No Red Sea. No defining moment where God's people stood trapped between an army and impossible waters. No miracle where God does the impossible and opens the waters before them.

The miracle required pressure. The deliverance required waiting. And obedience required refusing another route.

If the Israelites had said yes to fear…

Yes to compromise…

Yes to returning to Egypt…

Yes to an easier escape…

They would have missed the miracle entirely.

And that truth confronted me.

Because in seasons when hearts feel hard—when progress is slow, when obedience feels costly—the temptation is not rebellion. It's replacement. Replacement peace. Replacement joy. Replacement connection. Replacement certainty.

But saying yes too early often interrupts what God is doing beneath the surface. The Bible says "there is a time for everything, and a season for every activity under the heavens" (Ecclesiastes 3:1).

Obedience doesn't always feel peaceful at first. Sometimes it feels like loss. But the loss is not wasted. It is the very ground in which something new is being formed.

Pressure, Fire, and What Gets Formed

Diamonds are not formed in comfort. They are forged under extreme pressure, buried deep beneath the surface, unseen for years. Without pressure, carbon remains ordinary. Under pressure, it becomes something rare and brilliant. And sometimes—often—that pressure comes in the form of relationships.

Clay works much the same way. Before it can be shaped, it must be softened. Before it can be strengthened, it must pass through fire. The fire doesn't destroy the clay; it solidifies it. Without the fire, the vessel remains fragile, unfinished, unable to hold what it was created to carry.

In the same way, if we flee every season of pressure, we never become who we were meant to be. If we refuse the fire, we remain malleable but unformed. If we escape too early, we never see the brilliance God was shaping beneath the surface.

If I had run from my marriage every time my husband and I argued, or I didn't get my way, or I just didn't feel like being married, we would never have raised our children together or built a business together or shared fun memories together. I am a better me because of him, even when he gets on my nerves and I get on his.

Sometimes the bravest act of obedience is staying long enough to see what God is forming in you.

Staying, waiting, praying, and choosing alignment over escape doesn't mean you'll never struggle. It means you trust God more than your momentary feelings. It means you believe transformation is possible even when it's slow. It means you recognize that feelings fluctuate but covenant, character, and calling require endurance.

And when staying is no longer safe, Scripture does not shame leaving. God does not ask us to stay in a harmful situation when it is not ours to carry. Discernment is not about enduring pain for the sake of pain; it is about knowing when God is shaping you and when something is harming you.

I am still learning this. Still practicing it. Still surrendering my instinct to run when discomfort rises.

But I have learned this much. Not every door that opens is an invitation. And not every urge to leave is freedom. Sometimes the most courageous act of obedience is staying, and sometimes it is finally leaving. Discernment knows the difference.

Sometimes the most faithful thing you can do is refuse the exit and trust that what God is building in you is worth the wait.

REFLECTION

Marriage and long-term commitment ask something of us that almost nothing else in life asks: to stay present in difficulty without the guarantee of immediate resolution. Before you move forward, take an honest look at where you are tempted right now to say yes to, something that looks like relief but might really be escape. It may not be a dramatic exit. It may be subtle: emotional distance, quiet withholding, the way you have stopped praying for something because hope started to feel like too much to carry.

Think about the difference between happiness and joy—not as a theological exercise but as a personal one. Where are you chasing the feeling of relief in a place where God may be calling you to something deeper and more rooted? If you are in a season where staying is no longer safe, bring that honestly to God too. This chapter was not written to shame anyone into staying where harm exists. It was written to invite discernment. Ask Him directly: Am I being called to endure for the sake of what You are forming in me? Or am I being called to leave with courage and clarity? He is big enough for both questions. What He is not asking you to do is stay numb, stay hidden, or keep calling endurance what is actually just the absence of the courage to name what is happening.

PRAYER

Lord, You see the places where staying feels hard and leaving feels easier. You know the moments when my emotions speak louder than Your truth, when relief feels more appealing than obedience, and when walking away seems like the only way to stop the ache.

Give me discernment to know the difference between danger and discomfort. Between the seasons You are calling me to leave and the seasons You are forming me through. I do not always know the difference on my own. I need You to be clear, and I need the humility to listen even when the answer is harder than the exit.

Strengthen me to choose faith over impulse, obedience over relief, and trust over control. And when obedience feels costly, remind me that You have never abandoned anyone in the middle of a surrender You authored. Help me not to run. And if I must go, give me the wisdom to know it, the courage to move, and the grace to do so in Your timing not mine.

In Jesus' mighty name, amen.

My Reflections

Personal notes from Chapter Twelve

CHAPTER THIRTEEN

Practical Strategies for Saying No with Grace and Faith

By now, we've done the heart work.

We've explored why saying no can feel so threatening—how trauma can silence us, how fear of rejection can masquerade as kindness, how shame can keep us stuck in cycles of agreement we never intended. We've talked about God's yes, God's no, and God's not yet. We've sat with silence long enough to realize it isn't punishment, it's preparation. And we've learned that a rightly timed yes can unlock alignment, provision, and peace.

This is where all of that meets real life.

Because discernment without strategy can leave us frustrated. Conviction without tools can turn into guilt. And even the most spiritually mature "aha" moment can unravel quickly when your phone buzzes, your calendar fills, or someone you love looks at you with expectation in their eyes.

Urgency imposed by others is not the same as instruction given by God.

One of the biggest reasons no feels so hard is surprisingly simple: Our priorities are often unnamed.

When everything feels urgent, everything feels important. And when everything feels important, boundaries collapse. We end up saying yes not because we're called to, but because we can't quite articulate why we shouldn't.

Jesus never lived that way.

Despite constant demands—crowds pressing in, disciples asking questions, people needing healing—He refused to be ruled by urgency alone. Scripture tells us that very early in the morning, while it was still dark, Jesus slipped away to a solitary place to pray. That detail matters. He didn't wait until the day hijacked Him. He ordered His life before the noise began.

That one practice—anchoring Himself in the Father before responding to people—kept Him aligned. Even good needs didn't override God's order.

I had to learn this the long way.

For years, being available was my default setting. As a mother of six, a wife, a military veteran and spouse, and a leader in high-responsibility roles, dependability had become my identity. I said yes because I could. Because I had always figured it out before. Because people counted on me, and I liked being counted on.

What I failed to do was clearly name what mattered most to me in that season.

Once I began identifying priorities—spiritual, relational, professional—something shifted. Boundaries stopped feeling like rejection and started feeling like stewardship. Saying no wasn't about disappointing others; it was about guarding what God had entrusted to me.

Scripture tells us to guard our hearts because everything else flows from them. When the heart is unguarded, the overflow will be chaos—even if it looks productive on the outside.

And I'm preaching to the choir, but we live in a hurried society.

Decisions come at us constantly—texts, emails, opportunities, requests, notifications, deadlines. Everyone needs an answer, and they usually want it now. That fast pace alone creates pressure, and over time, that pressure produces something subtle but dangerous: decision fatigue.

When we are tired of deciding, we default to what feels easiest. Often, that's yes. Not because yes is right, but because no feels like work. And when we are worn down by constant deciding, discernment suffers first; we stop asking whether we should and start asking only whether we can. We stop asking, "Is this aligned?" and start asking, "How fast can I respond?" And speed, while efficient, is rarely wise.

Scripture warns us about this dynamic plainly. It tells us that while we may plan our course, God directs our steps. That means planning is not a lack of faith; it's part of faith. Careful planning, Scripture says, leads to abundance, while haste leads to loss. That loss is not always financial; sometimes it's relational, emotional, or spiritual.

When life feels rushed, the most spiritual thing we can do is slow down.

Take the beginning of the year, for example. Every New Year, we're drawn to the idea of a fresh start. We set resolutions, build vision boards, adjust habits, and imagine a better version of our lives. Sometimes we follow through. Sometimes we don't.

But the instinct to start over is God-given.

God calls His people to purpose. And purpose requires direction.

Why am I talking about vision boards and goal setting in a book about yes and no? Because vision gives context to decision-making. When you know where you're going, it becomes much easier to recognize what doesn't belong.

Scripture tells us to write the vision and make it plain—not so we can control outcomes, but so we can stay aligned. If you don't know what God is building in your life, every opportunity will feel like it might be from Him. And if you keep saying yes to things that don't align with the vision God is forming, you won't move forward; you'll move in circles.

God cannot fulfill plans you refuse to define. And it becomes very difficult to protect a direction you've never clarified.

Vision doesn't eliminate faith. It focuses it.

But to align our yeses and nos in the right way, we must first be more direct in our responses. If fear had a favorite word, it might be maybe.

Maybe sounds polite, gentle, non-confrontational. It buys time and keeps the peace—at least temporarily. But maybe is often just fear wearing good manners.

I used maybe a lot. Maybe I can help. Maybe that could work. Maybe; let me see.

What maybe actually did was keep other people waiting and keep me internally conflicted. It postponed honesty and prolonged anxiety. Most of the time, I already knew the answer. I just wasn't ready to say it out loud.

One of the most freeing shifts I made was learning to replace maybe with pause.

"I need time to pray about this."

"Let me review my current commitments."

"I can't answer that right now."

Those sentences felt uncomfortable at first. Slow. Inefficient. Unproductive. But urgency imposed by others is not the same as instruction given by God.

There is another layer we must name honestly: We are most likely to say yes when we are vulnerable, going through illness, divorce, grief, job loss, loneliness, fear, exhaustion.

Scripture reminds us not to lean on our own understanding during these seasons, not because God is withholding, but because pain is loud. Vulnerability is not the time for permanent decisions. It's the time for grounding, prayer, and support.

Instead of maybe, sometimes the most faithful response is not deciding at all—at least not yet.

This isn't about becoming rigid or unavailable. It's about becoming intentional.

It's about recognizing seasons. Reevaluating commitments. Understanding that what was once a faithful yes may now need to become a gracious no.

God is not offended by reevaluation. He often invites it.

When you live this way, decisions feel lighter. Relationships become clearer. And even when someone is disappointed by your no, you aren't undone by it because your yeses and nos are anchored somewhere deeper.

Training the Body to Say No

Let me start with a confession. I have been told more than once by more than one person to fix my face. Apparently, my face tells an entire story that I did not authorize it to tell. Someone will say something I find questionable and, in my mind, I am responding with grace. I am being measured. I am choosing my words carefully. And then someone leans over and says, "Fix your face." Every time, it catches me off guard. Because in my mind, I am the nicest person in the room. I genuinely try to speak with love. My face apparently does not always get the memo.

What strikes me about that is not just the expression itself; it is the unawareness. Someone else had to tell me what my face was communicating because I could not see it. I was completely unaware that I was looking at people with what I can only assume was visible disdain while believing I was being perfectly pleasant. That gap between what we think we are projecting and what we are actually projecting is exactly why practicing in a mirror matters. You cannot manage what you cannot see.

We spend a great deal of time preparing our minds and our spirits for difficult conversations. But the body also needs to be trained, because your mouth can say no while your face is apologizing for it. Your words can hold a boundary while your posture is already backing away from it. And the person on the receiving end will believe what your body says long before they process what your words meant.

Nonverbal communication is not a footnote to the conversation; it is often the conversation. Tone, posture, eye contact, and facial expression carry more weight in how a message is received than the words themselves, which means you can practice the perfect, grace-filled no and still undermine it entirely with a dropped gaze, a nervous smile, or shoulders that curl inward before you finish the sentence.

I used to practice saying no in the mirror. I am not embarrassed to admit that now, though I might have been then. And I want to be clear about why. It was not only about checking my face, though that mattered too. It was about getting in the habit of saying no at all. I had to tell myself no in the mirror enough times that I would start to believe it and then I'd be able to convey it. There is something that happens when you hear yourself say a thing repeatedly, steadily, without flinching. The word stops feeling dangerous. The sentence stops feeling like an offense. Your voice learns to carry it without asking for permission first.

I did it because I realized my body had never learned to hold steady while my mouth said something uncomfortable. I had said no while already reaching for an explanation. I had said no while my face was doing something that looked more like a request for forgiveness than a clear answer. The mirror showed me what I was actually communicating something—and it was not confidence. So I practiced. Calm voice. Steady eyes. Shoulders back. No trailing "but." No reflexive smile to soften the blow before the other person even had a chance to respond.

It felt strange at first. That strangeness is important information. It tells you that your body has been trained in a different direction—toward accommodation, toward apology, toward making the other person comfortable at the expense of your own clarity. You are not broken. You are simply practicing something new. And like any new skill, the discomfort is part of the process not a sign that you are doing it wrong.

What makes this particularly layered is that the settings where no feels most physically difficult are not always the ones you would expect. Many people assume that saying no is hardest when they are in a subordinate position—the employee facing a demanding supervisor, the volunteer facing a ministry leader who treats availability as devotion. And yes, that is genuinely hard. The power differential is real. The fear of consequence is real. We will talk about that directly in this chapter.

But some of the most disorienting nos happen in the opposite direction—when you are the one with authority and the no still won't come out clearly. Parents know this. You are the authority in the home. Your child is looking at you. And still, something in you hesitates because you want to be liked, because conflict feels costly, because you have spent years managing the emotional temperature of the house and saying no always spikes it. The position of authority does not automatically make it easy to say no. For many people, it makes it more complicated because the stakes feel higher, and the disappointment feels more personal.

The mirror exercise works precisely because it removes the other person from the equation entirely. There is no one to manage, no reaction to preemptively soothe, no relationship to protect in the moment. It is just you learning what your own no looks and sounds like when it is delivered without apology. Once you know what that feels like in a low-stakes setting, you have something to return to when the stakes are high.

Try it. Stand somewhere private and while looking at yourself say the following phrases aloud:

"I'm not able to take that on right now."

"That doesn't work for me."

"I need to pass on this one."

"No, but thank you for thinking of me."

Notice what happens. Does your voice drop at the end? Do you look away? Does a smile appear that you didn't intend to show? Do your shoulders shift? These are not flaws. They are the places where your body is still trying to protect you from a discomfort that the no itself would resolve. With practice, the body learns. The steadiness becomes available to you not just in the mirror but in the room, at the table, in the hallway, in the text message you finally send without rewriting seventeen times.

Training your body is not about becoming cold or immovable. It is about bringing your whole self into alignment with what you already know is true. Your words, your voice, your face, your posture. They all should be saying the same thing at the same time. That coherence is not intimidating. It is actually one of the most reassuring things another person can encounter because it means they can trust what you say. Your yes will mean yes. Your no will mean no. And both will be delivered by someone who has done the work to know the difference.

Saying No at Work Without Losing
Your Job, Your Mind, or Your Witness

Let's talk about the workplace, because that is where some of the most spiritually costly yeses happen.

You know the moment. Your supervisor sends an email—or worse, stops by your desk—and asks you to handle something that is clearly not your job. Maybe it belongs to someone who keeps dropping the ball and everyone knows it, but no one has addressed it. Maybe it has been quietly "reassigned" to you because you always figure it out. Maybe you have already said something, and here it is again anyway, dressed up like a favor.

Somewhere in your spirit, before you even finish reading the message, you feel it, that familiar tightening. That quiet voice saying, this is not mine.

Let me be honest with you. There are moments when I have wanted to ignore the request entirely. Pretend the email went to spam. Walk the long way around the building to avoid the conversation. And yes, there have been moments when the idea of hurling a stapler felt deeply satisfying. But that is not the godly way. And if we're being honest, it doesn't actually solve anything.

So what do you do when the workplace becomes one of the primary arenas where your yes is being taken for granted?

The first thing you do is slow down before you respond. The second thing is to refrain from overexplaining your no.

Again, Nehemiah didn't explain himself. He is the model to follow when we feel the need to explain our responses.

When you are asked to take on work that belongs to someone else, or to carry an assignment that does not align with your role, your first step is to name your great work—not defensively but clearly: "That falls outside the scope of what I'm currently responsible for. I want to make sure I can give my full attention to the priorities I've been assigned. Can we talk about who is best positioned to handle that?"

That sentence is professional. It is firm. It is not filler language, and it protects your witness. Don't overexplain yourself.

Now, sometimes the issue is more complex than a misdirected assignment. Sometimes the issue is the assignment itself, specifically, what it was designed to do to you.

There is a term that organizational researchers have used since 2005 to describe a phenomenon many women—and particularly Black women—have been living long before anyone named it: the glass cliff.

Unlike the glass ceiling, which keeps women out, the glass cliff lets them in—but into roles that are precarious, underfunded, or in crisis, often at the exact moment that success is least likely. Organizations appoint women to lead turnarounds. To fix what decades of mismanagement broke. To take on the project no one else wanted to touch. And then, when the impossible isn't accomplished in thirty days, the failure is quietly attributed not to the impossible conditions but to the person appointed to overcome them.

For Black women, this burden is doubled. We are not just carrying an impossible assignment. We are carrying the weight of expectation from people who want us to succeed and from people who are watching to see if we won't. Our outcome can be and often is, quietly framed as evidence against our entire gender, our entire race, our entire community.

That is a cross that no one person was designed to bear.

So when someone dangles an opportunity that feels too fast, too broken, or too politically convenient, discernment is not just wisdom. It is survival.

Before you say yes to any significant opportunity, ask the questions you are allowed to ask: What does success look like in ninety days? What resources are available? What is the timeline for realistic outcomes? Who has tried this before, and what happened to them? What support will I have?

You are not being difficult. You are being a good steward of the gift God placed in you. If those questions are unwelcome, if the hiring authority bristles at being asked what they mean by "success", that is important information.

God does not call us to positions where success requires His absence. He calls us into assignments He has already vetted and resourced. There is a difference between a divine stretch assignment—one that is hard because God is growing you and a human setup that is designed for you to fail. Both can feel uncomfortable. It takes discernment to tell them apart.

History gives us a powerful example of women who faced exactly this kind of assignment and refused to let impossible conditions become their legacy.

If you have not seen the Netflix film The Six Triple Eight, add it to your watch list. Better yet, read the history first.

The 6888th Central Postal Directory Battalion was the first and only all-Black, all-female battalion to serve overseas during World War II. In February 1945, they were sent to Birmingham, England—and later to Rouen and Paris, France—to address a crisis that had been building for years: seventeen million pieces of undelivered mail sitting in warehouses. There were letters to soldiers; packages from mothers, wives, and children; mail that had been piling up, disorganized and neglected for so long that some of it had been sitting in hangars since the war began.

The conditions they were sent into were not ideal. The facilities were inadequate. The discrimination they faced as Black women in a segregated military was real and relentless. They were given minimal resources, high expectations, and a timeline that military officials estimated would take six months.

They finished in three.

Working in three shifts around the clock, under the motto No mail, no morale, these women sorted and delivered mail that had been declared nearly impossible to process. They did not wait for better conditions. They did not wait for acknowledgment, equity, or applause. They focused on their assignment, and they executed it with excellence.

Their commanding officer, Major Charity Adams—and yes, I noticed the last name—was told by a general that she could be replaced with a white officer if she could not meet standards. Her response was steady and unshakeable: "Over my dead body, sir."

That is not a typical response, but it is close. And it was absolutely the godly response.

What the Six Triple Eight teaches us about the glass cliff is this: Not every impossible assignment is a setup. Some of them are a calling. The difference is not in the difficulty of the task. It is in the clarity of the assignment and the presence of God in the execution. Major Adams and her battalion did not succeed because the conditions were fair. They succeeded because their purpose was clear, their unity was strong, and they refused to let the chaos around them define what was possible within them.

That distinction matters when you are standing at the edge of your own impossible assignment.

The question to ask is not Is this hard? The question is, Is this mine? Is this the work God has prepared for me, in this season, for this purpose? Or is this an invitation to exhaust myself so someone else can avoid accountability?

Hard is not the same as wrong. But hard without calling will drain you.

When the Six Triple Eight accepted their assignment, they were not naive about what they were walking into. But they walked in together, anchored in purpose, carrying each other, focused on who was waiting for the mail they were about to deliver. They did not ask whether the task was fair. They asked whether the mission mattered. And when the answer was yes, they went to work.

That is discernment in action. It is not the absence of difficulty but the presence of clarity.

Daniel sat in a lion's den too, but he did not walk in alone. He "resolved not to defile himself" (Daniel 1:8).

Daniel made his decision before the pressure arrived. He did not wait until the moment of conflict to figure out where he stood. His no was already in place before anyone asked the question.

That is the preparation we need to do. You need to know where you stand before the email comes, before the meeting, before the opportunity is framed as now or never. Know what you will and will not carry. Know what season God has placed you in. Know what your great work is so that when someone tries to pull you off it, you already have the answer.

The hardest part of all of this is not the decision. It is the discernment—especially when everything around you is loud.

The workplace is loud. Expectations are loud. Pride is loud. Fear of missing out is loud. The opinions of people who benefit from your yes are very, very loud.

God speaks in a whisper.

Here is what I have learned: The whisper is always there. I was not always still enough to hear it. And I missed some things because of that. But God, in His mercy, meets us where our hearing has been trained.

If you are trying to hear God in the middle of a complex workplace decision—whether to take the promotion, to push back on the assignment, to say yes or no to the opportunity in front of you—the discipline is simple, even when it is not easy: Stop before you respond.

Don't just pause. Stop. Pray before you reply to the email. Pray before you walk into the meeting. Write the decision on paper and bring it to God before you bring it to your supervisor. Isaiah 30:21 promises that when you are aligned, you will hear a voice behind you saying this is the way; walk in it. But you cannot hear direction if you are already moving.

The Bible tells us to "trust in the Lord with all your heart and lean not on your own understanding; in all your ways submit to Him, and He will make your paths straight" (Proverbs 3:5–6).

The workplace is not exempt from that instruction. God is not only Lord over Sunday mornings. He is Lord over Monday's inbox and Thursday's performance review and the conversation you have been dreading for two weeks.

Bring it all to Him . . . before you decide.

Your no at work is not just about protecting your time. It is about protecting your assignment. And no one knows that assignment better than the One who gave it to you.

Deeper Reflection

Before you move into the prayer, take more than a moment with these questions. Get your journal. These are not meant to be answered quickly.

Do I know what season I am in, or am I responding to everything as urgent?

Urgency is not a season. It is a posture, and for many of us it has become the only posture we know. Before you answer this question, sit with it honestly, not the version of your life you present to others but the actual internal state you wake up with. Are you perpetually behind? Does rest feel like a luxury you'll get to eventually? If the answer is yes, that is not a scheduling problem; it is a spiritual one. What would it mean to name the actual season you are in right now, not the season you wish you were in or the season you are pretending to be in? Write it down and then bring it to God as an honest offering not a problem to fix.

Where in your professional or personal life have you been doing someone else's work and calling it faithfulness?

Think carefully before you answer. Sometimes we absorb the responsibilities of others so gradually that we no longer remember when they became ours. We covered for someone once, and then again, and then it became the expectation. We did not plan to carry this, but somewhere along the way our willingness became their permission. Where has that happened in your life, and what has it cost you not just in time or energy but in creativity, in joy, in the ability to do your actual assignment well? Write it down. Name the specific role or relationship. Then sit with this question: Is God asking you to release it, or are you holding on because releasing it would require a conversation you have been avoiding?

Have you ever been placed on a glass cliff, asked to carry something impossible, with the expectation of perfection and very little support?

If you have lived this, you already know the weight of it. The promotion that felt more like a trap. The opportunity that came with invisible strings. The assignment that was framed as an honor but quietly felt like a test for which you were not given the tools to pass. Take a moment to name that experience honestly. Write down what it felt like to stand at that edge. And now consider these questions: What did you do with it? Did you lean into God in that season, or did the noise of expectation drown out His voice? If you made it through, what did God teach you in the impossibility? If you are still in it, what would it look like to bring that specific assignment to Him today for clarity about what is yours to carry and what is not?

When you are in the middle of a decision at work, how often do you pause to pray before you respond, and what gets in the way of that pause?

Be specific and honest. Is it pride? Are you afraid that pausing makes you look uncertain or slow? Is it pressure? Do you feel that good leaders respond immediately? Is it habit? Have you simply never built the practice of bringing professional decisions to God before you act on them? What would it look like, practically, to change that this week, maybe not in every situation but in the next significant moment where you feel that familiar tightening in your spirit? What if you treated that tightening not as anxiety to manage but as an invitation to pray before you proceed? What might change?

What would slowing down before answering actually change in my life?

Don't think about this theoretically but specifically. Think of one decision you made in the last thirty days that you now wish you had brought to God first. What was the moment you said yes—or yes by silence? What would you have said if you had paused? This is not an exercise in regret. It is an exercise in awareness, because awareness practiced consistently becomes wisdom. And wisdom, as we have said from the very beginning of this journey, is worth pursuing at any cost.

My Reflections

Personal notes from Chapter Thirteen

CHAPTER FOURTEEN

When Others Don't Like Your No

One of the hardest truths about learning to say no is this: The people who benefited most from your yes will often struggle the most with your no.

Sometimes that resistance is subtle. It's a pause in the conversation, a raised eyebrow, a comment like, "You've never said no before." Other times it's more direct—disappointment, frustration, even accusation. Family members who are used to your availability may feel blindsided. Employers who have grown comfortable with your overperforming may push back. Friends who once praised your generosity may quietly resent your boundaries.

When the Church Can't Handle Your No

Sometimes it happens in church.

For many believers, saying no in a spiritual environment feels especially dangerous. We are taught to serve, to give, to sacrifice. We hear sermons about laying down our lives and dying to self. So when the Spirit prompts restraint, we can immediately wonder whether we're being selfish, unspiritual, or disobedient.

But Scripture is honest about this. It says obedience to God does not guarantee human approval—even in religious spaces.

Jesus lived this tension constantly.

People were not offended by His miracles; they were offended by His authority. He healed on the Sabbath. He withdrew from crowds. He refused to perform on demand. He didn't say yes simply because expectations were placed on Him.

At one point, after an intense season of ministry, Jesus slipped away to a solitary place. The crowds went looking for Him, eager for more teaching, healing, access. When they found Him, they expected Him to stay.

Instead, He said no.

He didn't say no because the need wasn't real, or the people didn't matter, but because His calling was clear. He told them plainly that He had to move on, that this was why He had been sent. In other words, He was saying your need is real, but it is not my assignment right now. Read that again. Your emergency is not my assignment right now.

That distinction matters.

In some churches availability becomes synonymous with faithfulness. Burnout is quietly praised as commitment. Exhaustion is reframed as sacrifice. And boundaries—especially when they disrupt a system—are subtly labeled as divisive.

You may hear well-meaning phrases like, "But this is ministry" or "We really need you" or "If God called you, He'll give you the strength." And sometimes those statements are true. But sometimes they are used—intentionally or not—to override discernment.

Even good leaders can struggle with your no. Not because it's wrong, but because it forces a recalibration. A role needs to be rethought. A schedule adjusted. A gap acknowledged that your yes had been quietly filling for a long time.

Scripture asks us a piercing question here: Are we seeking the approval of people, or the approval of God? It's not an anti-leadership question. It's a pro-alignment one.

Guilt vs. Conviction

One of the most difficult spiritual skills to develop is learning the difference between God's conviction and human expectation.

God's voice brings clarity even when the instruction is hard. It brings peace even when obedience is costly. Human pressure, on the other hand, brings urgency, guilt, and a constant fear of disappointing someone.

God is not a God of disorder. He does not lead through panic. If saying yes consistently robs you of peace, fractures your family, or pulls you away from what He has already entrusted to you, that is not obedience. It is imbalance.

I had to learn this personally.

There were seasons when my yes was celebrated, applauded, and even spiritualized—while my home quietly paid the price. When I finally said no, not everyone understood. Some people were disappointed. Some were frustrated. And yes, even within church spaces, the resistance was real.

But obedience is not validated by applause. It is validated by alignment.

Take Moses for example. Moses said no to Pharaoh again and again, even when compromise would have been easier. Jeremiah spoke truth no one wanted to hear and paid dearly for it. Paul refused to soften the gospel to maintain favor. Jesus Himself disappointed crowds, withdrew from expectations, and resisted pressure—even when people followed Him enthusiastically.

Jesus warned His followers that obedience might cost them approval, not because they were doing something wrong, but because they were doing something faithful.

This is not a call to be abrasive or confrontational. It is a reminder that obedience and popularity are not the same thing.

Sometimes when others don't like your no, it isn't a sign that you've missed God; it's confirmation that you're listening.

Obedience Doesn't Require Applause

So what do you do when people cannot handle your no? When others resist your boundaries, you are not required to overexplain, justify, or manage their emotions.

Sometimes a simple statement is enough: "I've prayed about this, and this is where God has me right now." Other times it sounds like: "I'm honoring the season I'm in" or "I can't commit to that at this time." And sometimes, wisdom looks like silence—because not every no requires a conversation.

Jesus said it plainly: let your yes be yes, and your no be no.

You are not responsible for soothing every disappointment. You are responsible for stewarding obedience.

But guilt, unfortunately, has a way of reopening doors God has already closed. It whispers things like, You're letting people down or You're not being Christlike or You should be able to handle more by now. But Scripture draws a clear line between conviction and condemnation.

Conviction guides. Condemnation pushes.

There is no condemnation for those who are in Christ Jesus. If what you're feeling drives you toward panic, self-doubt, or pressure rather than peace and clarity, it is not God calling you back. It is fear trying to regain control.

Learning to say no in spaces where yes is expected is one of the final refinements of discernment. It requires humility, courage, and trust. Trust that God sees what others don't. Trust that He will cover what obedience costs. Trust that alignment matters more than applause.

And sometimes, when others don't like your no, it isn't a sign that you've missed God. It's confirmation that you're listening.

Think about a woman I'll call Denise. Denise had sung on the worship team at her church for over a decade. She was gifted, consistent, and deeply committed—the kind of member whose voice anchored the team on Sunday mornings, who stepped into the lead role when others weren't available, who showed up even when her own week had been hard. The choir director counted on her. The congregation had come to expect her. And for a long time, Denise was glad to be needed.

Then her season changed. A new baby. A husband navigating a difficult transition. The quiet but undeniable sense that she was pouring from an empty place and calling it service. So she did what she believed was the right thing. She went to her choir director and asked to step back for a few months to tend to her home.

She expected understanding. What she received was something else entirely. The choir director didn't say anything overtly unkind. But the message came through in other ways—a comment about how the team depended on her, a suggestion that perhaps she was letting her personal life interfere with her calling, a barely veiled warning that the congregation would feel her absence. A few team members echoed the concern. One woman told her gently but pointedly that the Lord calls us to serve even in difficult seasons. And underneath all of it was an unspoken accusation that by stepping back, Denise was letting the entire ministry down. That without her, the choir would falter. That she was being selfish dressed up as responsible.

Denise nearly reversed her decision because the silence and the subtle withdrawal felt like confirmation that she had failed, that her no had cost her something she could never get back.

What Denise had to learn—and what this chapter is about—is that other people's discomfort with your no is not evidence that your no was wrong. It is evidence that they had quietly built something on your yes without ever asking your permission to do so. Denise did not belong to the choir. The congregation's experience of Sunday morning was not her personal responsibility to maintain at the cost of her own household. And the idea that her temporary absence would cause the church to crumble was never about the church. It was guilt being used to keep her in place.

Denise eventually returned to the worship team in her own time and with a clarity about her calling she hadn't had before. Her no didn't end her ministry. It protected it. And when she came back, she came back whole.

Maybe you are not on a worship team. Maybe you have never sung a note in your life. But ask yourself: Is there a role, a responsibility, or a relationship where you have become so load-bearing that the people around you have stopped asking whether you are okay and started assuming that you always will be? Where your presence has gone from a gift to an expectation and where stepping back, even briefly, is treated not as wisdom but as betrayal? Have you stayed in that role not because God called you to stay but because someone made you feel that leaving would mean the whole world—or at least their world—would fall apart without you? Have you continued to serve out of guilt? Has that guilt become the thing keeping you in a season God already released you from?

REFLECTION

When we establish a new boundary, there is often a grace period before the real test arrives. The test is not whether we can say no once. It is whether we can hold it when the people who benefited from our yes push back. Before you move forward, think about a boundary you have set—or tried to set—that was met with resistance, not from an enemy but from someone whose disappointment genuinely mattered to you. How did you respond? Did you hold the boundary, overexplain it, weaken it, or abandon it entirely? And what did that response cost you not just relationally but in how you see yourself?

Consider whose disappointment you are currently carrying that God never asked you to manage. Who in your life seems to have an unspoken agreement with you that your yes is their right? And how has managing their disappointment been quietly shaping the decisions you make not based on what God is saying but based on what they need you to say? Think about Denise. Maybe your choir is a team at work, a volunteer role at church, a family expectation, a friendship that has never learned to receive your no without punishing you for it. Is there a space in your life where you have stayed not because God called you to stay but because leaving felt like proof that you had failed? What would it mean to release that story and trust that God can hold what you are setting down?

PRAYER

Lord, strengthen me to obey You even when others do not understand. When my no is met with frustration, with disappointment, or with the kind of spiritual language designed to make me question my own discernment, anchor me not in defensiveness but in the quiet certainty that You have heard what I have prayed and seen what I have surrendered.

Help me release the need for approval not because relationships do not matter but because my obedience cannot remain hostage to someone else's comfort. Teach me the difference between feedback that sharpens me and pressure that is simply asking me to go back to being what I no longer am.

Teach me to say no with humility, knowing that I am not always right, that discernment is always a work in progress, and that holding a boundary is not the same as closing my heart. Anchor my confidence in Your voice alone. And let that confidence be quiet, steady, and unshaken by applause or its absence.

In Jesus' mighty name, amen.

My Reflections

Personal notes from Chapter Fourteen

CHAPTER FIFTEEN

The Freedom of a Well-Placed No

The art of saying no often feels like loss in the moment.

It can feel like walking away from opportunity, recognition, or approval. It can feel like choosing the long road when a faster one is right in front of you. It can feel like sacrifice. And if we're honest, sacrifice rarely feels noble while we're in it; it usually just feels inconvenient, uncomfortable, or unfair.

But over time, I've learned a counterintuitive truth: Every obedient no carries the seed of a greater yes.

God has never wasted a surrendered decision in my life. Not one.

There were seasons when saying no meant slower advancement, fewer accolades, and choices that made little sense to people watching from the outside. I have felt the tension of those moments deeply. At the time, those decisions felt like loss. Later, they revealed themselves as protection, preparation, or positioning.

Jesus captured this paradox perfectly when He said that unless a kernel of wheat falls to the ground and dies, it remains only a single seed. But if it dies, it produces many seeds (John 12:24). That wasn't poetic language meant to sound comforting. It was instruction.

What Jesus was really teaching us is something we resist with everything in us: Growth requires release.

A seed held safely in your hand stays intact. It can be admired, protected, even cherished. But it never becomes a harvest while it is being held.

A seed only fulfills its purpose when it is released into the ground, where it breaks open, loses its original form, and disappears before it multiplies.

In your hand, a seed is preserved.

In the ground, a seed is transformed.

Jesus was teaching us that multiplication requires burial. What feels like dying to ourselves is often God positioning us for growth we cannot see. And this is where my own story began—long before titles, leadership, or public platforms.

I grew up on the South Side of Chicago with my mom, my sister, and my grandmother. My mother was a single parent until I was twelve years old. We were not wealthy by any measure. My mom worked hard to make ends meet, and for a season we relied on food stamps. There were no safety nets—only determination, prayer, and a household held together by resilience.

The neighborhood I grew up in changed over the years. It became rougher. Harder. More fragile. A boy was killed in the alley just down the street from where I lived.

By every statistic that society uses to predict outcomes, I should have become one.

People expect girls who grow up in neighborhoods like mine to follow a certain path: Multiple children. Multiple fathers. Limited opportunity. Sometimes addiction. Sometimes incarceration. Sometimes invisibility.

It is an outdated stereotype, but it is still one that quietly shapes expectations. And some of those expectations were delivered not from a distance but up close, from peers, from institutions, from people who looked like me and from people who didn't.

My sister and I had opportunities that a lot of kids on our block didn't have. My mother made sure of it. One of them was Girl Scouts camp, and I mean real camp, the kind where you are away for a stretch, sleeping in bunks, learning things that had nothing to do with the block we went home to. We experienced things like tennis, horseback riding, activities that, to our neighborhood, belonged to a different world entirely.

When we came home and talked about those things, we were treated like pariahs.

Tennis? Horseback riding? Those were not things Black kids were supposed to want or enjoy or even know existed. The message, though never spoken plainly, was clear: You think you're better than us. We didn't. We were just kids who went to camp. But the rejection stung anyway because it came from our own community, the people whose acceptance should have been guaranteed.

And then there was the other kind of rejection. The kind that didn't even come with confrontation.

I spoke properly. I used correct grammar, enunciated clearly, and did not adjust my speech based on who was in the room. And on my block, that meant I talked white. Which meant I was different. Which meant, in the social economy of childhood, that I was suspect.

There were no invitations. No one knocked on our door to ask if we wanted to play. The exclusion was quiet and total—a silence that is louder than any insult because at least an insult acknowledges that you exist.

Those are the nos that are hardest to name, the ones carried in a turned back, a group that walks away when you approach, a childhood block where you are perpetually on the outside looking in not the ones thrown at you directly.

I was quieter then. Shyer. And quiet, shy girls on hard blocks sometimes look like easy targets.

So I had to fight, not because I wanted to or because I was aggressive or angry or looking for trouble but because doing nothing was not an option. And when you are a girl who would rather read than argue, some people interpret that as an invitation. They were wrong.

My sister saved me more times than I can count. She was my front line, my backup, my person. I learned early that God does not always deliver you from the hard season alone. Sometimes He gives you someone to stand in it with you. For me, that person was my sister.

I was attending a mixed-race school at the time, and there was an opportunity to advance a grade. I was already working in the higher-grade curriculum. The academic fit was there. The readiness was there. Everything pointed toward yes.

Except that I had gotten jumped, and I had fought back.

And because I had defended myself—not started a fight but finished one—I was deemed too immature for advancement. The opportunity was taken away. The very intelligence and capability that should have opened the door was not enough to overcome the fact that I had refused to be victimized without retaliating.

That one hurt differently.

It was confusing in the way that only institutional rejection can be confusing to a child. I was being told simultaneously that I was smart enough to move ahead and too unruly to be trusted with the opportunity. The message underneath the decision was something I would spend years learning to name: You can be capable, but if you don't stay in the shape we've decided you belong in, we will find a reason to say no.

I was twelve when we moved to the suburbs. New city. New school. New soil. I thought the hard season was behind me.

I was wrong—but only for a season.

When I arrived at my new school, I was placed in remedial classes. Every single one. Remedial reading, remedial math, all of them. The lowest level available. Despite having already read the books assigned in those classes. Despite having scored well—very well—on the state reading and math tests. Despite every measurable indicator saying I did not belong there.

And when I told my teacher I had already read the books, she looked at me with the expression of an adult who has decided before a child speaks that what the child is about to say is probably not true.

I was told in language that a child absorbs rather than fully processes in the moment that I did not look like I belonged in honors classes.

Let that land for a moment.

I had been punished in my previous school for fighting back when I was jumped, because they thought I was too much. Now I was being held back at my new school because the perception was that I was too little. Not enough. Not the right image. Not what smart was supposed to look like.

Both rejections used me against myself. Both tried to make me smaller than I was. And while both were wrong, they still impacted me.

I spoke up. I told my mother what was happening, and that was not a small act. Speaking up when you are new, when you are already navigating an unfamiliar environment, when the adults around you have already formed an opinion, that takes courage. It is the kind of courage that does not feel brave in the moment. It just feels necessary.

My mother went to that school. She asked to see my scores. And the moment those numbers were placed in front of the people who had placed me in remedial classes, I was moved to honors. Overnight. The same child. The same brain. The same girl who did not "look" smart on a Monday was apparently quite smart enough by Tuesday.

Nothing changed except who was advocating in the room.

That lesson stayed with me. I was not bitter—I made peace with it long ago—but I gained clarity. The clarity that systems will tell you no for reasons that have nothing to do with your actual capacity. That institutions will try to contain what God has already released. And sometimes the most powerful thing you can do is speak up, bring your receipts, and let someone who loves you stand in the room while the truth is being read aloud.

At a young age, I was planted in circumstances that could have buried me.

I could have accepted the label. I could have agreed with what people assumed my life would become. I could have said yes to becoming what others quietly expected of me.

But even then—before I understood theology, calling, or purpose—I was being planted not buried.

God was already doing something underground.

A seed does not get to choose the soil it is placed in. But it does grow according to the life that was placed inside of it.

Every rejection, every silent exclusion, every institution that said you don't look like what we're looking for, none of it could touch the life God had put inside of me. They were trying to determine my ceiling. God was building my foundation.

Some seeds must fall for identities to survive.

Earlier in this book, I shared how multiple career opportunities came before the timing was right. On paper, they were impressive. In reality, they created strain. There was tension in my marriage. There was a lack of peace, a quiet sense that something sacred was being threatened.

I didn't want to say no. I wanted to move forward. But God's silence—and my husband's hesitation—were signals I could not ignore.

Looking back, I see that God wasn't withholding opportunity. He was protecting covenant.

Had I rushed ahead simply because the door was open, I might have gained a title and lost a foundation. That no, spoken reluctantly and with tears at the time, became the burial that preserved my marriage and strengthened it for the season that followed.

What felt like delay was actually mercy.

Leadership has a way of tempting us to hold on tightly.

We are praised for decisiveness, productivity, and availability. We are rewarded for saying yes quickly and often. But there is a subtle danger in confusing control with stewardship. Anything I refuse to surrender limits what God can do through me.

A seed that never falls never multiplies.

In leadership, saying no to ego, pace, or public pressure can feel like stepping backward. But in God's economy, surrender always comes before expansion. Humility precedes promotion. Preparation comes before platform.

Trusting God's timing means believing that delay is not denial and silence is not neglect. It means trusting that God sees the whole picture—your family, your health, your marriage, your calling—not just the opportunity in front of you.

As someone who values efficiency and dislikes wasted time, learning to wait was humbling. But waiting taught me discernment. It taught me dependence. And it taught me that God's pace is protective.

When God asks us to wait, He is often doing deep work underground, where roots grow before fruit appears.

A well-placed no makes room for rest. It makes room for joy. And it makes room for God.

There is a freedom that comes when you stop trying to carry everything.

A well-placed no rooted in prayer, aligned with Scripture, and guided by peace does not constrict your life. It expands it. You stop living reactively. You stop negotiating your values. You stop mistaking a full schedule for a faithful one.

For me, that freedom has looked like deeper presence with my family, greater clarity in leadership, and a faith no longer fueled by exhaustion. It has meant choosing depth over breadth and obedience over applause.

A well-placed no makes room for rest. It makes room for joy. And it makes room for God.

And sometimes, the no God asks of us is not about opportunity but about people.

This is the part that hurts the most.

There have been seasons when God removed people from my life—friends, connections, relationships I expected to carry forward with me. The separation was unexpected, painful, and confusing. I didn't understand why it had to happen that way.

Not every ending was my choice.

What was my choice was whether I trusted God in the removal. Because when relationships end without explanation, our instinct is to fix, to understand, to smooth things over, to chase clarity, to reopen doors God may have intentionally closed.

That urge is human. It is natural. And I have given into it before. I have chased closure. I have asked for conversations God did not authorize. I have tried to rescue relationships that were already being released. And every time I did, I felt the same thing afterward—not peace but distraction.

Spiritual maturity does not mean you don't care when people leave. It means you learn when not to chase what God is removing. Wisdom teaches us that not every ending needs explanation and not every loss needs correction.

Sometimes restraint is the obedience.

If a relationship, friendship, or connection is meant to be restored, God is fully capable of doing that without your chasing, negotiating, or forcing it. What is from God does not require your anxiety to sustain it.

Our role is not to figure it out. Our role is to remain obedient where we are.

David understood this.

Long before he became king, David was isolated in the wilderness. Anointed, yes, but hidden. Promised, yes, but pursued. God removed him from familiarity and placed him in obscurity, not as punishment but as preparation. The wilderness stripped David of excess—relationships, comfort, predictability—until all he had left to lean on was God.

That season shaped the king David would become.

When I eventually went to Washington, DC, I experienced a similar kind of isolation. I was separated from my family during the week. Away from familiar support systems. Navigating high-pressure environments that felt like a proverbial lion's den.

It was in that isolation that God spoke to me more clearly than He ever had before.

I went home to a quiet apartment. I had more time alone with God. I had no choice but to lean on Him. And along the way, I lost people who were no longer meant to walk with me into that season.

I didn't understand it at first. I asked God what I had done wrong. And instead of correction, I sensed Him saying: This is a wilderness season. To get through it, you must cut through the overgrowth and let Me be your primary source.

Letting go was painful. Lonely. Necessary.

Not everyone can go where God is taking you. And not everything that leaves is a loss. Some things are being buried so that something greater can grow.

Sometimes the most courageous act of obedience is staying, and sometimes it is finally leaving. Discernment knows the difference.

And sometimes the most courageous thing you can do is open your hand — not because letting go is easy, but because you trust the God, who asks you to.

REFLECTION

Where has God asked you to release control or let go even when you didn't understand why? Think about a specific moment—not a general feeling but an actual season or decision. What was being removed, and what did you do with the space it left behind? Did you immediately try to fill it, or did you sit in the discomfort long enough to ask what God was doing? If you are still in the middle of the releasing, write about what it feels like to hold on and what it might feel like to open your hand.

There is a difference between seeking wisdom and seeking control. Wisdom asks God what He is doing and waits in faith. Control asks God to explain Himself and then negotiates. Where in your life right now are you chasing something—a conversation, an explanation, a restored relationship, a reopened door—that God may have already closed? What would it mean to stop chasing it, not because you don't care but because you trust the One who closed it? And finally, what is the one faith-based no—not a fear-based no but one rooted in trust—that is still waiting to be spoken in your life? What would it take to speak it this week?

PRAYER

Lord, teach me to trust You not only with what I choose to release but with what You remove without explanation. Remind me that every no I have received—from You, from others, from circumstances that closed before I was ready—has been working something in me that I could not have built through comfort alone.

Where I have been chasing what You have already closed, give me the grace to stop. Where I have been grieving what You have taken, give me the faith to trust that You are not careless with what You carry away. A seed that is surrendered is not lost. It is planted. And You are faithful with what is planted in You.

Teach me the freedom of a well-placed no. The freedom that comes when I stop trying to hold open every door and start trusting that the right ones are held open by You. Let my surrendered decisions become the very ground where something new begins to grow—something I could not have imagined while I was still holding on.

In Jesus' mighty name, amen.

My Reflections

Personal notes from Chapter Fifteen

CHAPTER SIXTEEN

The Wisdom of Holy Restraint

For many of us, silence feels uncomfortable—sometimes even wrong.

We were raised to believe that good people respond. They explain themselves. They smooth things over. They make others feel comfortable. Silence, on the other hand, can feel rude, dismissive, or unloving. It can feel like failure, like we dropped the ball in a conversation we were supposed to manage.

But Scripture tells a different story.

There are seasons when God does not call you to act. He calls you to hold. Holy restraint is the discipline of choosing silence not out of fear, avoidance, or indifference but out of discernment and obedience. It is the wisdom to recognize that not every question deserves an answer, not every demand requires engagement, and not every provocation warrants a response. "There is a time to be silent and a time to speak" (Ecclesiastes 3:7).

Learning when not to respond may be one of the hardest spiritual disciplines, especially for those of us who are conscientious, empathetic, or conditioned to manage other people's emotions. Silence asks us to trust God with outcomes we would rather control with words.

When Silence Is Strength

Jesus modeled holy non-response repeatedly—and intentionally.

When falsely accused before Pilate, Scripture tells us that Jesus made no reply, not even to a single charge. Pilate was amazed—not because silence was expected, but because it was powerful. Jesus was not confused. He was not afraid. He was not powerless. He was discerning.

Later, when brought before Herod, who questioned Him at length, eager for spectacle—Jesus again chose silence. No explanation. No defense. No performance.

Jesus understood something we often forget: Engagement gives power. Silence, when guided by God, preserves it.

Every response is an investment. Jesus did not invest His words where truth would not be received. He did not explain Himself to people who were committed to misunderstanding Him. That was not avoidance. That was wisdom.

Why Silence Feels Dangerous

For many people—especially women, leaders, caregivers, and trauma survivors—silence feels unsafe.

We fear being misunderstood. We fear escalation. We fear being labeled rude, cold, or unkind. Some of us learned early that silence led to punishment, or that our worth was tied to responsiveness. Others were taught that explaining ourselves was the price of being accepted.

So we overexplain. We justify. We respond too quickly, too fully, too often.

Scripture gently frees us from that burden. Proverbs 26:4 says, "Do not answer a fool according to his folly, or you yourself will be just like him." Then, almost immediately, Proverbs 26:5 says the opposite: "Answer a fool according to his folly, or he will be wise in his own eyes."

Placed back to back, these verses are not contradictory. They are instructional. They teach discernment. Sometimes silence is wisdom. Sometimes response is necessary. The difference is not politeness. It is purpose.

Knowing When Not to Respond

Holy restraint is not ghosting, passive aggression, or avoidance. It is intentional, prayerful, and grounded in peace.

There are moments when you've already answered and continuing to engage would only reopen a door God has closed. Someone keeps pressing you to serve, give, or volunteer beyond your capacity, even after you've said no. In those moments, silence reinforces the boundary you already established. You stop reexplaining. You stop defending. You simply do not reenter the conversation.

There are other moments when a message arrives that is not meant to get a reaction. It could be a text, email, or comment designed to provoke guilt, anger, or defensiveness. You feel it immediately, the tightness in your chest, the urge to respond quickly and fix things. Holy restraint pauses. It prays. It waits. And sometimes, it does not respond at all because clarity was never the goal.

Then there are questions asked in bad faith. Requests for "understanding" that are really attempts to control the narrative. Jesus encountered this often. He recognized that explanation would not bring peace. Silence became stewardship.

And sometimes, it's someone familiar—someone who knows your weakness for overexplaining—pushing again, hoping your discomfort will reopen the door. In those moments, the absence of engagement teaches what words never could.

Silence is not empty. It is instructive. But is silence disrespectful? Not when God is leading it. Silence becomes disrespectful only when it is rooted in contempt. Holy restraint is rooted in clarity, peace, and obedience. It trusts that God can defend, clarify, or close the door Himself.

"In quietness and trust is your strength" (Isaiah 30:15). This verse reframes everything. Silence can be an act of trust, a declaration that you do not need to manage every reaction, correct every misunderstanding, or rescue every conversation.

Stillness is not weakness. It is strength
under control.

Silence as Obedience

There were seasons in my own life when silence was not avoidance. It was survival.

Silence preserved my marriage. Silence guarded my calling. Silence allowed God to speak without the noise of others' expectations. Had I responded to every invitation, every demand, every opinion, I would have forfeited peace for approval. Because of my positions as a public figure, I often had to exercise restraint and bite my tongue. For many years my tongue bled with restraint.

Holy restraint taught me that obedience does not require explanation.

Stillness is not weakness. It is strength under control.

REFLECTION

Holy restraint—the discipline of silence when speech feels more natural—is one of the hardest spiritual practices to develop, precisely because it asks us to trust an outcome we cannot control with words. Before you move forward, identify a specific situation where you feel pressure to respond—a conversation, a relationship, a conflict, a demand—where you sense that God may actually be inviting you to be still instead of explaining, defending, or fixing. What is it about that situation that makes silence feel so risky? Is it the fear of being misunderstood? The discomfort of watching someone draw their own conclusion? The deep, conditioned belief that your worth depends on your responsiveness?

Think about a time when silence served you, when not responding was, in retrospect, exactly the right thing. What did that silence teach you? And what would it look like to draw on that memory now in the situation where silence feels most costly? Consider what you are most afraid will happen if you remain silent. Write it down if you can. Look at it plainly. Is that outcome as likely as fear tells you it is? And even if it is, is it yours to prevent? Scripture says that "the Lord will fight for you; you need only to be still" (Exodus 14:14). In this particular situation, what would it actually look like to let Him do that?

PRAYER

Lord, teach me the wisdom of restraint. Not the restraint of someone who has nothing to say, but the restraint of someone who trusts that You are more than capable of defending what I choose not to defend myself.

Free me from the belief that silence is surrender. That not responding means I am losing something. That my value depends on my visibility or my willingness to explain myself in every room. Remind me that Jesus stood before Pilate and said nothing, and that silence was not weakness. It was authority. And it was enough.

Where I am tempted to reenter conversations You have already closed, hold me back. Where a message is designed to provoke and a silence is the most faithful response, give me the peace to offer it without apology. Anchor me in the truth that in quietness and trust is my strength. That stillness is not passivity; it is power under Your authority.

In Jesus' mighty name, amen.

My Reflections

Personal notes from Chapter Sixteen

CHAPTER SEVENTEEN

From Permission to Commission: Living What You've Learned

By the time we reach this point, something important has already happened.

You no longer need permission.

We have examined the many reasons saying no feels so difficult. We traced those struggles back to early conditioning, trauma, fear of rejection, misplaced responsibility, spiritual misunderstanding, and even exhaustion masquerading as faithfulness. We explored Scripture's consistent use of boundaries and discovered that God's no—and even His silence—are not signs of distance but expressions of care. We learned that discernment is not weakness, restraint is not failure, and obedience is rarely loud or flashy.

In other words, you have already been given permission. Permission to rest. Permission to pause. Permission to say no without apology. Permission to stop negotiating your worth through overextension.

But permission was never the destination.

Permission is where healing begins. Commission is where obedience matures.

From Permission to Commission

At some point, discernment must move from internal understanding to external living. The art of saying no is not meant to remain theoretical. It is meant to be practiced in conversations, in decisions, in leadership, in relationships, and in the quiet moments when no one is watching but God.

Commission is what happens when clarity turns into responsibility.

You are not being commissioned to say no to everything. You are being commissioned to say no to what does not align, does not belong, or does not honor the season God has placed you in. You are being commissioned to stop outsourcing discernment to urgency, guilt, fear, or approval. You are being commissioned to live awake, to choose intentionally rather than reactively.

This is where the shift occurs.

When No Becomes Leadership

Early in this journey, saying no may have felt like self-preservation. And in many ways it was. Boundaries protected wounds that were still healing. Silence guarded places that needed restoration. Restraint created space for clarity to return.

But now, saying no becomes something more.

It becomes leadership.

Whether you lead a household, a team, a ministry, a classroom, a courtroom, or simply your own life, your decisions teach others what is permissible. When you honor rest, you teach others that rest is holy. When you refuse pressure, you teach others that urgency is not authority. When you decline what is misaligned, you make room for others to do the same.

Your obedience creates culture and habit.

This is why Scripture never treats discernment as optional. Jesus did not merely teach truth; He modeled restraint. He withdrew when crowds demanded more. He remained silent when engagement would have distracted from purpose. He said no to premature crowns, illegitimate power, and misaligned timing. And in doing so, He showed us that obedience is not passive, it is intentional.

Commission does not require perfection. It requires faithfulness.

You will still get it wrong sometimes. You will still hesitate. You may still say yes when you should have waited, or wait when you should have moved. That does not negate the commission. It refines it. Discernment is not about flawlessness; it is about alignment over time.

You Are Being Sent Out Free

What matters now is this: you no longer live at the mercy of pressure.

You do not owe access to everyone who asks. You do not owe explanation for every boundary. You do not owe exhaustion as proof of faithfulness.

You owe obedience to God and to be a good steward of what He has entrusted to you.

Commission means you now carry responsibility not only for your own peace but for the example you set. For the way your children learn what rest looks like. For the way your colleagues learn what healthy leadership sounds like. For the way your community learns that holiness is not found in depletion but in discernment.

This is the work ahead.

Not louder faith—but wiser faith. Not faster obedience—but truer obedience. Not endless yeses—but surrendered decisions.

You have permission and now you have purpose.

And as you move forward, remember this: every well-placed no makes room for a better yes. Every obedient pause protects something sacred. And every decision offered to God—whether affirmation, refusal, or silence—can become an act of worship.

You are not being sent out burdened.

You are being sent out free.

REFLECTION

You have come a long way. Before you step into what comes next, take a moment to mark this threshold honestly—not with a to-do list but with real acknowledgment of how you have been changed by what you have read, wrestled with, and sat with in these pages. Where were you when you opened this book? What did you believe about yourself, your boundaries, and your right to say no? And where are you now, even if it is only slightly different, even if the shift is more internal than visible, even if you still have more questions than answers?

Commission is not perfection. It is willingness. So sit with this: What is the one pattern, one relationship, one habit, one yes that has been quietly costing you, that you are ready, truly ready, to bring to God and release not because you have it all figured out but because you have learned enough in this journey to trust that He is faithful with what you surrender? And consider who is watching you—not to pressure you but to remind you that discernment is never only personal. Your children. Your colleagues. The younger woman who is learning what obedience looks like by watching how you live it. What do you want her to learn from watching you? And what would it take to begin living that, starting today?

PRAYER

Lord, as I close this chapter and step forward, I bring You all of it. The yeses I have given away and should have guarded. The nos I have withheld and should have spoken. The seasons where I moved too quickly and the ones where I waited too long. I bring them without shame, because I know You already know them.

Thank You for not giving up on my discernment when I did. For staying patient with my process. For meeting me in my confusion with clarity I did not always deserve and guidance I did not always follow. I am not finished learning. I do not expect to be. But I am further along than I was, and that is enough for today.

As I move forward, commission me not for perfection but for faithfulness, not for constant yeses or absolute nos but for the kind of discernment that keeps returning to You before it answers anyone else. Let my life be a quiet testimony of what it looks like to belong to You. To live anchored, discerning, and free.

In Jesus' mighty name, amen.

My Reflections

Personal notes from Chapter Seventeen

Choosing Discernment, Living Free

In The Art of Saying No While Staying in the Will of God, we have traced the long and often complicated relationship we have with affirmation and refusal. We began by examining where our fear of no was formed—through early conditioning, spiritual misunderstanding, trauma, and the quiet belief that our value is measured by how much we give, endure, or produce. Along the way, we returned again and again to Scripture and discovered that God has never treated boundaries as optional. His nos, His delays, and even His silences are not punishments; they are protection.

We confronted the emotional weight that often follows refusal—guilt, shame, fear of rejection, and the desire to be seen as faithful, helpful, or indispensable. We named how unhealed wounds can distort discernment, how busyness can masquerade as obedience, and how leadership without restraint eventually collapses under its own excess. We learned that peace, not pressure, is often the clearest signal of God's direction—and that obedience is not proven by exhaustion.

One of the most sobering truths we uncovered is one Scripture makes clear but culture rarely names: Unchecked yeses can become a form of spiritual gluttony. When we consume affirmation, productivity, comfort, and approval without discernment, our hearts become weighed down not through rebellion but through excess. Jesus warned against this not because it is dramatic but because it is subtle. A heart burdened by too much is just as impaired as one hardened by disobedience.

Writing this book over nearly four years changed me. It slowed me down. It corrected me. It forced me to revisit moments where obedience had been rushed, delayed, or diluted. I learned that discernment is not a destination we arrive at once; it is a discipline we practice daily. And freedom is not found in doing more but in choosing wisely.

If there is one truth I hope remains with you, it is this: You were never called to live depleted, overextended, or ruled by appetite. You were called to live anchored—obedient, discerning, and free. Every yes is meant to be intentional. Every no is meant to be prayerful. And every decision, when surrendered to God, can become an act of worship.

What comes next is not permission—you already have that. What comes next is responsibility.

Responsibility to listen before you agree. Responsibility to pause before you explain. Responsibility to discern before you decide.

This is where maturity shows up.

Maturity is not measured by how much you can handle. It is measured by how well you steward what God has already entrusted to you. It is the ability to resist urgency without becoming passive, to hold conviction without becoming rigid, and to say no without becoming hardened or unloving. It is the willingness to disappoint people when obedience requires it, and the humility to accept that not everyone will understand your restraint.

One of the hardest lessons I had to learn is that obedience does not guarantee affirmation. Sometimes obedience produces distance. Sometimes it produces misunderstanding. Sometimes it produces loneliness. And sometimes it produces silence—both from others and, for a season, from God Himself.

But silence does not mean abandonment. Delay does not mean denial. And a closed door does not mean you have failed.

Often, it means God is doing work you cannot yet see.

We also encountered biblical figures who understood this truth deeply. David learned it in the wilderness. Moses learned it in obscurity. Jesus lived it in restraint. Each of them was formed not only by what they were allowed to do but by what they were required to refuse. Their authority did not come from constant action; it came from alignment.

That alignment is what discernment protects.

Discernment guards your heart from making permanent decisions based on temporary emotions. It keeps you from mistaking discomfort for disobedience and urgency for instruction. It reminds you that not every open door is an invitation and not every opportunity is holy ground.

It also reminds you that God is not in competition with your peace.

If saying yes consistently costs you peace, something is misaligned. If obedience always feels frantic, something is off. God may stretch you, but He does not rush you. He may call you to sacrifice, but He does not call you to live perpetually depleted.

This matters because many of us were taught—directly or indirectly—that holiness looks like availability and that faithfulness looks like exhaustion. We internalized the idea that rest is earned, boundaries are selfish, and discernment is optional. But Scripture tells a different story.

Jesus withdrew.

Jesus rested.

Jesus refused.

Not because He was unloving but because He was aligned.

He knew who He was, where He was going, and what He was sent to do. And because of that clarity, He could say no without explanation and yes without fear.

That is the kind of clarity God desires for us.

As you close this book, you may feel affirmed, challenged, unsettled, or even convicted. That is okay. Growth often begins with discomfort. But let that discomfort draw you toward God not away from Him. Let it invite you into deeper listening rather than defensive justification.

You do not need to overhaul your life overnight. Discernment is rarely loud or dramatic. It often begins with one small pause. One prayer before responding. One moment of silence instead of explanation. One boundary honored instead of overridden.

And you will not get it right every time. I haven't.

You will sometimes say yes too quickly.

You will sometimes say no too late.

You will sometimes realize in hindsight what you missed in the moment.

That does not disqualify you. It refines you.

God is not waiting for perfect discernment. He is inviting faithful posture. A posture that says, I am willing to listen. I am willing to wait. I am willing to obey—even when it costs me.

And when it does cost you, remember this: nothing surrendered in obedience is ever wasted.

Not time.

Not opportunity.

Not relationship.

Not effort.

God redeems what is released to Him.

Some of the nos you will speak will feel like endings. Others will feel like protection. Some will feel heavy. Others will feel freeing. And some will feel both at the same time. But each one, when offered prayerfully, will create space for the right yes to follow.

Because discernment is not about shrinking your life. It is about clarifying it.

It is about living with integrity rather than impulse, with alignment rather than appetite, with wisdom rather than fear.

And ultimately, it is about trust.

Trust that God sees what you do not.

Trust that He understands the full cost of your obedience.

Trust that He is capable of opening doors no one can close—and closing doors no one should reopen.

You are not behind.

You are not failing.

You are not less faithful because you have learned to say no.

You are becoming wise.

And wisdom—quiet, steady, anchored wisdom—is one of the greatest gifts God gives to those who are willing to listen.

FINAL PRAYER

Lord, I come to the end of this book not because I have mastered everything it has asked of me, but because I am more willing than I was when I began. More willing to pause. More willing to listen. More willing to say no to what drains me and yes to what You have actually called me to.

May the decisions I make from this day forward reflect Your truth. Let every yes be intentional and every no be prayerful.

Guard my heart from excess. Guard my schedule from urgency that masquerades as Your calling. Guard my relationships from the slow erosion that comes when I give what I do not have to people who have not been given the right to require it.

Teach me to walk in discernment and freedom not as a destination I arrive at once but as a daily posture I return to, every time I am tempted to choose approval over obedience. When obedience feels costly and restraint feels misunderstood, remind me that You are with me in every decision, not just the dramatic ones but the ordinary ones too. Anchor me in Your peace. Align me with Your will. And let my life be a quiet testimony of what it looks like when someone stops performing and starts trusting.

In Jesus' mighty name, amen.

My Reflections

Personal notes from Conclusion

About the Author

Zaneta Adams is an ordained minister, Emmy Award–winning producer, licensed attorney, and Retired US Army disabled veteran. But before any of those titles, she is a woman who has had to learn—sometimes the hard way—what it means to say no while staying in the will of God.

Her life has been shaped by seasons of sacrifice, obedience, and hard-won discernment. She served eight years in the US Army, National Guard, and Reserve before being medically discharged with honor. She has navigated the demands of a legal career, public service leadership at the state and federal level, and over two decades of ministry—all while being a wife and mother.

She is the founder and former president of WINC: For All Women Veterans, a nonprofit she built out of her own experience of being a woman whose voice and needs were often overlooked. Her advocacy for women—veterans and otherwise—runs through everything she does.

Zaneta has been married to Joseph Adams, also a US Army veteran, for over twenty-six years. Together they are the proud parents of six children, including two sets of twins. She knows firsthand what it costs to pour yourself out for others—and what it means to finally learn that obedience and depletion are not the same thing.

The Art of Saying No While Staying in the Will of God is her debut book.